HOW TO LIVE A LONG AND HEALTHY LIFE

HOW TO LIVE A LONG AND HEALTHY LIFE

ISBN (paperback): 978-1-968919-52-8
ISBN (ebook): 978-1-968919-32-0

Armin Lear Press, Inc.
215 W Riverside Drive, #4362
Estes Park, CO 80517

HOW TO LIVE A LONG AND HEALTHY LIFE

The Art and Science of Longevity

Harry L. Munsinger, J.D., Ph.D.

CONTENTS

INTRODUCTION

Average human life expectancy remained stable for thousands of years before beginning to increase in the seventeenth century, driven by advances in sanitation, nutrition, science, and medicine that reduced mortality among infants, children, and adults. Historians and anthropologists estimate that ancient humans lived an average of thirty-five years, based on studies of fossilized human bones and research on !Kung tribes of the Kalahari Desert near the Nambian border. The !Kung tribe of hunter-gatherers has been isolated from modern civilization for thousands of years; so anthropologists studied them to gain an understanding of what life may have been like for ancient hunter-gatherer tribes in ancient times because the !Kung lived in a way similar to how ancient humans survived before the agricultural revolution began ten thousand years ago. According to reports, the tribe was thriving. They had adequate food, appeared to be happy, developed strong family connections, and had ample leisure time because their lifestyle required only about 20 hours of work per week to obtain enough food, make clothing, and build shelters. The tribe did not, as Thomas Hobbes famously wrote, live in a "state of nature" that was "solitary, poor, nasty, brutish, and short." However, when anthropologists asked members of the tribe how old they were, they did not know. That was surprising, because recording individuals' ages began among the Babylonians in the fourth millennium BCE.

Based on estimates, the experts believed !Kung tribal members lived an average of around thirty-five years. Anthropologists have also studied ancient fossilized human bones to estimate the average age of early humans and concluded that their life expectancy was around 33 years. Thus, ancient hunter-gatherers probably lived approximately the same number of years as !Kung tribesmen and seventeenth-century Englishmen. It was not until the 1600s that scientists began systematically examining the life expectancy of the English population by collecting data on how long people lived and their causes of death. Later research showed that, with a few exceptions, average longevity has increased over the last three centuries, so that a child born today can expect to live nearly 80 years, about 45 years longer than ancient humans or seventeenth-century Englishmen did. Wars and pandemics temporarily reversed the upward trend of human longevity. Still, overall, life expectancy has increased steadily over the past three centuries, allowing people today to enjoy longer, healthier lives. Improved sanitation, advances in medical care, the development of hospitals, the discovery of vaccines, modern safety regulations, and adequate food have given modern humans many extra years of life. You might expect this increase in life expectancy to continue at the same rate in the future, so hundreds of years from now, the average life expectancy of humans might be one hundred forty years. However, that's unlikely because most of the increase in longevity over the last three hundred years resulted from more infants surviving childhood.

Modern adults are living longer than they did hundreds of years ago because infants and children are not dying at such high rates from infectious diseases or malnutrition. Over the last few centuries, advances in medical science have doubled the life expectancy of adults while increasing that of children by a factor of *ten*. Better nutrition, improved sanitation, and effective vaccines allowed humans to live longer. Artificial fertilizers (which increased food production), sewer systems (which reduced the spread of infectious diseases), and vaccines (which protect children against life-threatening diseases) contributed most to increased human longevity. Fertilizers, sewers, and vaccines have saved billions of lives, while the development of antibiotics, seatbelts, refrigeration, chlorination, pasteurization, and blood transfusions has saved only millions of lives. Until the seventeenth century, scientists knew little about life expectancy and had no effective methods for studying the causes of death and factors that increased longevity.

Studying Life Expectancy. The earliest recorded calculation of human life expectancy was published by John Graunt, who collected mortality data and published his results in 1662 in a work titled *Natural and Political Observations Mentioned in a following Index and made upon the Bills of Mortality*. Historians believe Graunt began his work to alert London authorities about outbreaks of infectious diseases such as bubonic plague or cholera, and to document the health of London's population. He systematically recorded causes of death, whether by murder, infectious disease, malnutrition, or old age. Graunt also used his mortality tables to estimate the existing population of London, concluding that there were likely about 384,000 inhabitants in the city at that time. His estimate was fairly accurate, because modern demographers believe the population of London in the 1660s was around 400,000. Based on Graunt's work concerning life expectancy, he was invited to join the Royal Society, a group of famous English scientists. Soon after his work was published, other countries began collecting mortality data on their populations.

The first theoretical analysis of life expectancy appeared in 1669 in letters exchanged between Dutch scientists Christian and Lodewijk Huygens. Lodewijk decided to calculate the average life expectancy of populations so London companies could offer life insurance to individuals at a fair rate, because the cost will be lower if people lived an average of fifty years rather than thirty-five. Lodewijk and Christian based their studies on the estimated life expectancy of populations rather than the number of years one individual would live because the results were more accurate. The first evidence that it was possible to increase the life expectancy of humans appeared in the mid-eighteenth century when demographers began collecting mortality rates separately for the English upper and lower classes. These data showed that English aristocrats had higher life expectancy than the general population. Longer life expectancy among upper class Englishmen suggested that it might be possible for all humans to live longer if they had access to adequate food, better housing, and medical care. However, until modern times only wealthy countries enjoyed increasing average life expectancy; today most people around the world are living longer. However, the causes of increased longevity are not so simple as early physicians believed. For example, early physicians attributed the longer average life expectancy of upper-class Englishmen to improved medical care, but that was not the case. Modern physicians have concluded that early medical techniques often did more harm than good to patients.

For example, King George III of England was "treated" with arsenic, which caused poisoning and probably shortened his life. Moreover, bloodletting was prescribed as late as World War I to treat influenza, although there is no reliable evidence that it actually increased longevity. Moreover, modern medical scientists believe bloodletting may have weakened or killed patients. It was not until the 1930s that Thomas

McKown, a British Canadian physician, realized physicians were not recording whether the treatments they prescribed to patients were helping them recover. He decided to study the effect of various treatments on patients' longevity to see if physicians were effective in prolonging human life. During his studies, McKeown found that the population of England had begun to increase years before physicians discovered effective cures for any illness, suggesting that something other than medical care was causing people to live longer at that time. He eventually showed that increased human longevity was due to the development of vaccines that were preventing childhood deaths from infections rather than because medical or surgical treatments prescribed by physicians were curing patients. Scientists have discovered that genetics and the environment jointly influence longevity.

For example, children of parents who live past one hundred are likely to live longer than the general population, and improved diet, sanitation, and medical care contribute to longer lives. Physicians have also discovered that people living in certain areas called Blue Zones live much longer than the general population. These Blue Zones are found in Sardinia, Okinawa, Loma Linda, Ikaria, and Nicoya. Individuals in Blue Zones exercise naturally, minimize stress, avoid obesity, eat a healthy diet, and have good social connections with family and friends. Inherited diseases, such as sickle cell anemia, cystic fibrosis, Tay-Sachs disease, hemophilia, Huntington's disease, and muscular dystrophy limit human lifespan. However, individuals who receive annual medical exams also live longer than people who don't visit a physician regularly. Annual physical exams assess current health, detect medical problems, allow early treatment, and extend human life. A diet rich in cheese, fish, fresh fruits, vegetables, grains, nuts, olive oil, and chicken reduces the risk of cancer, high blood pressure, heart disease, and strokes. Staying active also increases life expectancy.

Exercise maintains strength, cardiovascular fitness, mobility, and extends longevity. To maximize the effect of exercise, individuals should alternate strength training with aerobic exercise. Moreover, having a social network of family and friends significantly decreases the risk of developing a heart attack, Type 2 diabetes, depression, and Alzheimer's disease. Surveys show that employees are working longer today, so they need to maintain their skills to remain employable in an evolving job market. If current trends continue, freelance workers will outnumber corporate employees in another generation. Wealthy people live longer than the poor because they have access to health care, exercise, and eat a healthy diet. Having money contributes to living longer, but it's not the only factor associated with longevity. If you want to live longer, choose your parents carefully, make healthy lifestyle choices, and visit your physician regularly.

1

HISTORY OF LONGEVITY RESEARCH

Research into London mortality rates intensified after cholera first arrived in 1832 and triggered recurring epidemics that killed thousands. Dr. John Snow believed cholera was caused by contaminated water rather than "miasma" (an unpleasant atmosphere) and set out to prove his theory by collecting data associated with cholera deaths. First, he searched for the pathogen causing cholera in samples of water from London wells, but the microscopes available at the time were not powerful enough for Snow to see the bacterium, *Vibrio cholerae,* that causes the disease. In 1854, he decided to investigate whether an outbreak of cholera was linked to contaminated drinking water from a specific London well. Snow wanted to see if cholera cases were concentrated around the well. He began by plotting the distribution of cholera deaths in London and found that deaths were concentrated around a single well located at 40 Broad Street, London. When the local parish board agreed to remove the pump handle from that well, deaths from cholera cases in the area fell dramatically, proving Snow's theory that the disease was caused by contaminated drinking water rather than bad air. Snow's work led to the development of epidemiology, the study of how often infectious diseases occur in populations, why they occur, how to prevent them, and how to manage them once they occur.

Epidemiology. Epidemiologists study the incidence of diseases in different groups and why people become ill. The systematic study of cholera began in 1866, following an outbreak in the northern suburbs of London. The physician and statistician William Farr began collecting data on cholera deaths and studying the characteristics of persons who died from the disease. Farr's work led to the founding of epidemiology when he discovered that the life expectancies of upper-class Londoners were increasing, while the life expectancies of lower-class Englishmen living in London were not. He set out to learn why ordinary Englishmen were not enjoying the longer life expectancy of wealthy Londoners by applying statistical methods developed to understand life insurance pricing. Farr believed these statistical methods could be applied to public health and would lead to a better understanding of what causes cholera epidemics and how to stop them. He collected the cause of death, occupation, and age of Londoners who had died. Farr's goal was to find ways to prevent cholera epidemics, because he believed that preventing illness was easier and more effective than treating patients once the disease had developed.

He began by studying the relationship between cholera deaths and occupation, locality, and season to see if these factors influence mortality rates. Farr's goal was to improve public health and prevent epidemics. He collected data and developed mortality tables to understand trends in London death rates. Farr produced what are now called life tables, which show mortality rates for various age groups, and used these tables to compare the longevities of different populations. He knew that children often die from infectious diseases during infancy, so he believed it was essential to separate mortality rates by age to understand what was causing deaths among various groups in London. Farr's life tables enabled him to understand the health of an entire population, broken down by age, occupation, and location. He was born and raised in the country but practiced medicine in London, the largest city in England, so Farr compared mortality rates of urban and rural dwellers to see if there were significant differences in life expectancy between these groups. His first report analyzed the "Diseases of Town and Open Country" by studying the death rates of individuals living in London, Liverpool, and Surrey.

Rural and Urban Differences. Farr's results showed that people living in rural Surrey, where population density was low, drinking water was pure, and the air was clean, were likely to live longer than people residing in large cities such as London or Liverpool, with crowded living conditions, contaminated water, and smog. He found that country people had an average life expectancy of around fifty years, while individuals living in London died on average at age thirty-five, and those living in the squalid industrial city of Liverpool died at an average age of only twenty-five years. Farr's data showed that living in crowded cities is detrimental to public health, and some urban environments are more dangerous than others, especially for children. He concluded that industrialization and crowding in cities created major public health issues and recommended that London officials address the problem by improving living conditions in urban slums. Farr found that people living in the country exceeded the historical average life expectancy of thirty-five years, but people crowded into a dense industrial city such as Liverpool had an average life expectancy that was approximately ten years below the historical average of thirty-five years. He also found that during epidemics, mortality rates increased by around 30 percent during the early stages of the crisis, leveled off, and then began to decline, in a way similar to the curve of a projectile fired from a cannon. Named Farr's Law, this insight was the first known mathematical description of the course of an infectious disease. Based on his studies, Farr concluded that to improve public health, sewage should be separated from public drinking water to avoid epidemics.

Sewers. Drs. Snow and Farr discovered that bacteria in drinking water cause disease and convinced London authorities to build a separate drainage system to keep raw sewage from contaminating London's drinking water, because discovering that cholera was caused by contaminated water was only the first step in preventing epidemics. Public health authorities also needed to develop a way to separate drinking water from raw sewage to fix the problem. The solution was to build an integrated drainage system to keep raw sewage away from drinking water. The London sewer system was one of the outstanding engineering achievements of the age. Managed by Joseph Bazalgette, the project replaced a disorganized, inefficient drainage system developed piecemeal throughout London with an organized system of sewer lines that ran more than 80 miles under the city streets. The project was completed in six years and eventually saved millions of lives. However, building a system to keep sewage separate from drinking water was not a complete cure for infectious disease, because bacteria could still contaminate drinking water in other ways. To better protect public health, scientists suggested adding a small amount of chlorine to drinking water to kill any bacteria that might contaminate it, and heating beer, wine, and milk to kill bacteria that cause spoilage or contamination (pasteurization).

Chlorination and Pasteurization. It was difficult to estimate how large an effect adding chlorine to drinking water had on increasing human longevity, because at the same time chlorination was introduced, governments began requiring that producers pasteurize beer, wine, and milk before selling it to the public. As a result of these two simultaneous improvements in public health procedures, the mortality rate among children in America dropped by more than 60 percent. Still, scientists didn't know how much difference chlorine in water and pasteurization of beer, wine, and mile was making, because they were both introduced at nearly the same time. However, by taking advantage of the fact that some cities introduced chlorine into their drinking water later than others, David Cutler and Grant Miller estimated that chlorination accounted for approximately two-thirds of the decrease in mortality rates among children, and pasteurization accounted for the remaining improvement. In the nineteenth century, raw milk could be deadly to children if it was contaminated. In 1850, the problem was so prevalent that President Zachary Taylor died after drinking a glass of contaminated milk.

Cow's milk became a source of nourishment for children thousands of years ago, and when cattle were fed on open pastures, the milk was generally safe to drink.

However, the geography of New York City made it difficult to raise dairy cows on pasture close enough to transport fresh milk to households before it spoiled, because refrigeration had not yet been developed, and horse-drawn wagons were slow. Enterprising dairy farmers believed they had found a way around this problem by feeding dairy cows warm "mash" produced by local whiskey distillers in pens that were located close to the city. By feeding an inexpensive byproduct of distilling to dairy cows, farmers could keep their dairy farms close to New York City and deliver fresh milk daily to residents. However, feeding dairy cows "mash" from whiskey distilling resulted in the cows being crowded into small stalls where they became malnourished and diseased.

The milk produced by these cows was so pale that dairy farmers adulterated it with chalk, flour, and eggs to make it appear more like "pure country milk." The demand for cow's milk increased in New York City because women were entering the work force, they could not nurse their children while at work, and there were not enough wet nurses available to feed all the babies. As a result, cow's milk was substituted for wet nurses to feed the babies of working mothers.

Pasteurization. Cow's milk sold for six cents a quart in New York City at that time, and the lower classes began buying it for their children. Substituting cow's milk for a wet nurse was satisfactory so long as the raw cow's milk was pure, but if it became contaminated, the milk could be deadly for babies. After farmers began feeding "mash" to their dairy cows, children in New York City started dying at an alarming rate, and no one understood why. The cause of these deaths was discovered in 1854 by Louis Pasteur, when he began studying why beer and wine spoil. Using an improved microscope, Pasteur was able to see yeast organisms responsible for fermentation in beer and wine, as well as other organisms that were spoiling the beer and wine. Pasteur's work produced the germ theory of disease, even though he was primarily interested in finding a way to keep beer and wine fresh. He discovered that heating wine or beer to around 130 degrees Fahrenheit prevented the beverages from spoiling, and the process did not significantly change their flavor. However, pasteurization of milk, as the process was called, did not become standard practice in America until 1915. This life-saving procedure came to America because Robert Milham Hartley, a member of the Presbyterian Church, studied squalor in New York City slums and made recommendations about how to improve the lives of poor people in the city.

During his studies of the poor in New York City, Hartley investigated dairy producers and published a book titled *An Historical, Scientific, and Practical Essay on Milk: As an Article of Human Sustenance; with a Consideration of the Effects Consequent Upon the Present Unnatural Methods of Producing it for the Supply of Large Cities.* He analyzed the mortality rates of children in large cities using the methods of Snow and Farr. He showed that milk sold to poor New York City families was produced under unsanitary conditions. However, the United States government did nothing about Hartley's expose because it had no legal authority to regulate the dairy industry at that time. It was not until May 1858, when *Frank Leslie's Illustrated Newspaper* published an expose of New York dairies, showing they sold contaminated milk that was dangerous to the health of New York City children that authorities finally acted. The New York Academy of Medicine investigated the issue and found that "swill milk" was associated with increased infant mortality among New York Cities' poor families. Public outrage made it impossible for authorities to allow these dangerous urban dairies to continue operating, but no one knew how to fix the problem. Milk from upstate New York farms often spoiled during the summer while it was being transported to New York City, causing illnesses and death among children. In the 1880s, the emergence of the germ theory of disease made it clear that diseases such as diphtheria, typhoid, and scarlet fever were caused by microbes in milk and water. The problem was, how can you eliminate germs from milk safely and inexpensively?

One solution was to keep milk cold, and Frederic Tudor built a thriving business supplying ice for New York City to keep milk cold and fresh. But refrigeration was only part of the solution. Milk contaminated with bacteria could still be deadly to children, even if it was cold. To alleviate this problem, federal inspectors began visiting dairy farms and testing for bacteria in cows' milk. In 1906, the Food and Drug Administration was authorized by Congress to regulate food and pharmaceuticals.

As a result, the federal government finally had the authority to test and ban contaminated products.

Thanks to Pasteur's discovery of germs, authorities knew that heating milk would kill bacteria, making it safe for children to drink. But how could they convince the public that pasteurized milk was safe? The answer came from an unlikely source. Nathan Straus, who was born in Bavaria, moved to America before the Civil War and settled in the South. However, he was driven to bankruptcy by the war and moved to New York after it ended to start a new career. Straus prospered in the north after he co-founded Macy's Department Store and began improving living conditions among his employees. He opened shelters and distributed free coal to his workers during winter months. Straus had lost two of his own children to disease, and in conversations with Dr. Abaham Jacobi, another German immigrant, he learned about pasteurization. Using this information, he founded a laboratory to study pasteurization of milk on an industrial scale and began selling pasteurized milk to the poor below cost to improve children's health.

The *New York Times* ran a story about Straus' milk pasteurization, and as a result, he was appointed health commissioner of New York City. Soon after he was appointed, Straus learned of an orphanage on Randall's Island in the East River where almost half the children were dying annually. He recognized that because the children were isolated, they were a natural population for an experiment to prove that pasteurization of milk was safe and effective. Straus supplied pasteurized milk to these isolated children, without changing any other part of their diet. The mortality rate among these isolated children dropped significantly after they began drinking pasteurized milk. Once Straus proved pasteurization made milk safe for children, he began a national campaign to stop the sale of unpasteurized milk. However, the dairy industry opposed his efforts because pasteurization increased their costs. Straus' work attracted the attention of President Theodore Roosevelt, who ordered a government study of the health benefits of pasteurized milk. Experts concluded that pasteurization would save lives, so by 1920 the sale of unpasteurized milk was outlawed in America. Today, the Food and Drug Administration inspects and regulates the food and pharmaceutical products Americans consume.

Food and Drug Administration (FDA). The FDA changed how medicines are approved and sold in America. Before the agency was established, the United States pharmaceutical industry was unregulated and there were no restrictions on what could be offered as medicine to the public. In 1901, the Bureau of Chemistry was created by Congress, but it was only authorized to ensure that the chemicals listed on a bottle of medicine were present. It could not regulate their safety or efficacy. The problems created by this system of regulation became clear in the 1930s, when the German pharmaceutical company Bayer AG developed sulfanilamide (sulfa), an early antibiotic that saved millions of lives. However, because the drug was not soluble in alcohol or water, it had to be administered as a pill, which was difficult for children to ingest. To solve this problem, Samuel Massengill dropped out of medical school and formed a company to produce liquid sulfa for the American market. His chief chemist dissolved sulfa in diethylene glycol (a solvent similar to modern antifreeze) and added raspberry flavoring to make the liquid palatable so children would drink it. The liquid sulfa was effective in treating children's illnesses, but ethylene glycol is toxic, so children and adults began dying after drinking the sulfa elixir manufactured by Massengill's company.

Members of the newly established FDA did not know how to discover what was causing these deaths, but a chemist at the University of Chicago administered the sulfa elixir to animals and showed that ethylene glycol was killing the adults and children. By the time the FDA removed Massengill's sulfa elixir from the market, seventy-one adults and thirty-four children had been killed by ethylene glycol in the sulfa elixir. Congress held hearings and discovered that the FDA had no authority to test drugs for safety or efficacy, but only for chemical content. The legislature gave the FDA additional authority to require pharmaceutical companies to prove their products were safe and effective before selling them to the public. To standardize the testing of a drug's safety and efficacy, scientists developed the randomized, double-blind test to differentiate between the "placebo" effect, which occurs when patients take a sugar pill, and the effect of an experimental drug that actually cures the disease.

The Double-Blind Experiment. This research design requires that a group of patients suffering from an illness be separated into an experimental and a control group. The experimental group receives a new test drug, while the control group receives a pill of equivalent size, color, and shape, but without the new drug. Results from the control group establishes how long individuals require to recover without the new test drug, (called the placebo effect) while the results from the experimental group show whether the new drug is effective in treating an illness. If there are no significant differences between the experimental and control group, that means the drug is not effective. However, if the group that received the new drug recovers more quickly, the drug is proven effective. In double-blind studies, no one knows ahead of time which patients are in the experimental group and which are in the control group, so no psychological bias can influence the results. When the experiment is finished, the data are analyzed statistically to determine whether there is a significant difference between the control and experimental groups. By

1962, the FDA began requiring pharmaceutical companies to prove their products were safe and effective before they could be marketed. Beyond pasteurization, chlorination, and pharmaceutical regulation, another major scientific advance that increased the longevity of humans was the introduction of artificial fertilizers which increased the amount of food available to feed a growing population.

Synthetic Fertilizer. Some scientific discoveries have unintended consequences. For example, who imagined that learning how to convert nitrogen from the air into ammonium nitrates would produce artificial fertilizers that allowed farmers to feed billions more people? In 1908, the German chemist Fritz Haber began exploring how to synthesize nitrates. The industrialist and chemist Carl Bosch used Haber's laboratory procedure to design an industrial process to change atmospheric nitrogen into ammonia using heat and an iron catalyst. Germany used the Bosch process during the First World War to produce ammonia for munitions. After the war, farmers began adding synthetic ammonium nitrate to their fields, and the crops they planted produced more food. No other discovery has caused a larger increase in human longevity than artificial fertilizer. Before the introduction of synthetic fertilizers, farmers added animal manure to their fields, and microorganisms enriched soils by decomposing plants and animals, releasing ammonia in the soil. Mined bat guano was a primary source of natural fertilizer before chemists learned how to change atmospheric nitrogen into ammonia. However, manure and natural decomposition were unreliable and inadequate fertilization processes, so farmers were having difficulty growing enough food for a rapidly expanding population. Moreover, because of continuous use, soils became depleted, crops failed, and famines recurred. Additionally, unreliable rainfall, soil erosion, and the destruction of food and irrigation systems during wars limited food production for growing populations.

Recurring famines killed thousands, causing people to migrate in search of food.

For example, historians believe that the Mayan civilization was destroyed by an unusually long drought that caused crop failures, famine, death, and economic decline among that population. Ancient Egypt experienced famines when the Nile River failed to overflow for several years in a row, leading to social chaos. In the 1300s, the Little Ice Age brought unusually cold weather to Europe causing famines that killed an estimated one-third of the existing population. In addition to death, chronic malnutrition limited the labor individuals could perform, slowing economic growth and expansion.

Following the development of artificial fertilizer, the average height of humans increased several inches because of better nutrition. Synthetic fertilizers and more efficient production of meat from chickens, pigs, and cattle, increased the amount of food available to feed humans, which increased the health and size of the human population dramatically. The discovery of synthetic fertilizer doubled the carrying capacity of the earth, allowing the human population to reach eight billion and reduced the incidence of malnutrition from 30 percent in earlier generations to around 10 percent today. In 1928, Alexander Fleming discovered penicillin, which killed bacteria and saved millions of lives.

Antibiotics. Fleming recognized that penicillin could kill germs when he saw one of his culture plates had become contaminated with an unknown mold which inhibited the growth of bacteria in the dish. He grew the mold in beef broth and found that the liquid extracted from the mold killed germs causing scarlet fever, pneumonia, gonorrhea, meningitis, diphtheria, and strep throat. Fleming published his findings in the *British Journal of Experimental Pathology* and continued trying to purify and manufacture the antibiotic for years with limited success. In 1940, he saw an article in *The Lancet* entitled "Penicillin as a Chemotherapeutic Agent," authored by research scientists at the William Dunn School of Pathology at Oxford University. The Oxford group had discovered how to produce penicillin in larger quantities, successfully experimented with the antibiotic on animals, and showed it halted the growth of a staphylococcal infection in a human patient. Fleming, Florey, and Chain shared the Nobel Prize for their work on penicillin, which saved millions of lives. Another factor that has increased the average human life expectancy has been auto safety regulations.

Auto Safety. Soon after the development of the automobile, public health officials began recording automobile accidents as a cause of death. Autos proliferated on the roads of America, and as a result, deaths from vehicle accidents increased dramatically. By the early 1950s, auto accidents had become a significant cause of mortality in America. Since 1913, when statistics on auto deaths were first collected, more than four million Americans have been killed in auto accidents. More people have died in car crashes than from all the wars fought by the United States since it was founded. By 1955, with the introduction of the Interstate Highway system, millions of Americans were traveling at such high speeds that when there was an accident, the passengers were often killed. At that time, seat belts, recessed steering wheels, and crumple zones were not available on cars, and there were no airbags, anti-lock braking systems, headrests to prevent whiplash, or dashboard padding. To lower death rates from auto accidents, traffic lights were installed in America after 1914, speed limits were posted, and roads were designed to make them safer. But for years, no one paid attention to the basic design of the automobile to make it a safe container for passengers.

<u>Auto Safety Design.</u> The first person to seriously consider whether it might be possible to design cars that were safe to drive was Hugh

DeHaven. He was an American Air Force cadet on a training flight that ended when two planes collided. DeHaven survived, but was seriously injured, while the other pilot was killed in the crash. During his long recovery, DeHaven realized there was something about the design of his plane that allowed him to survive while the other pilot perished. He decided to discover how to manufacture a safe container for people who were moving at high speed. DeHaven decided to study how to design a cockpit that would help pilots survive a crash. He began his work by dropping eggs from the top of a building in different containers to understand how packaging could protect the eggs from breaking. By 1940, DeHaven was able to drop an egg off a ten-story building without damaging it. Dropping eggs off buildings is still a standard exercise among physics students at high schools, colleges, and universities. DeHaven published his research in a 1942 paper titled, *Mechanical Analysis of Survival in Falls from Fifty to One Hundred Fifty Feet.* His paper focused on eight case studies of people who had survived falls from varying heights and detailed the factors that enabled them to survive.

DeHaven concluded that the human body could survive a force of two hundred times the pull of gravity for short intervals so long as the gravitational force acted perpendicular to the long axis of the human body. He recommended that manufacturers design an automobile so it would reduce and distribute impact and pressure over the human body, allowing drivers and passengers to survive a crash. He believed, according to the laws of physics, that it was possible to design a car so that its passengers could survive severe auto accidents if the auto body was properly constructed and the passengers were wearing seat belts that would keep them inside the vehicle. Other scientists learned of DeHaven's work and began studying how to design safer packages for people. An engineer at the United States Aeromedical Research Laboratory, John Stapp, began studying what happens to the human body during rapid deceleration. He designed dummies that simulated the effects of deceleration in humans and built a rocket sled that traveled on rails and could be stopped in a few seconds from a speed of 120 miles per hour. Stapp and others rode the rocket sled while their bodies were connected to sensors that measured various forces affecting them. He made history while riding a sled at over 600 miles per hour, stopping in under 2 seconds, and surviving. Stapp was bruised and temporarily blind after the ride, but he survived the experience with no permanent injuries. He also proved that a pilot could be ejected from a jet flying at six hundred miles per hour and survive if the cockpit was designed correctly.

Based on his experience with the rocket sled, Strapp showed auto manufacturers how to build a safer car. In 1955, Ford introduced safety door latches, lap belts, a padded dashboard and sun visors, and a recessed steering wheel in their cars, but customer interest was low when these safety features were introduced. Moreover, General Motors, Ford's most serious American competitor, believed that highlighting the dangers of auto accidents was a bad idea for car companies and did not support the development of safer cars. General Motors executives seemed right because Ford's safety features didn't sell when they were first introduced. In 1959, Swedish car maker Volvo introduced the first successful safety device in cars when it designed and built a three-point seatbelt with lap and chest straps, which minimized soft-tissue stress and was easy to attach by snapping the belt into a single retainer. Tests showed that the three-point seatbelt reduced traffic mortality by 75 percent, preventing many deaths in car crashes. Volvo generously made the seatbelt design available to all auto manufacturers at no cost. However, American car manufacturers resisted adding safety features to their cars until Ralph Nader published his best-selling book, *Unsafe at Any Speed: The Designed in Dangers of the American Automobile.* After Nader's expose, car buyers began demanding safer cars. In 1966, Congress created the Department of Transportation to oversee automobile safety standards. The result has been that the number of deaths per one hundred million miles driven dropped from six in 1955 to one and one-half in 2018.

Summary. In 1854, Dr. John Snow began studying the link between cholera and contaminated drinking water. He found that cholera deaths were concentrated around a single well in London, but when the local parish board removed the pump handle, deaths from cholera fell dramatically, proving Snow's theory that the disease was caused by contaminated water. Snow's work led to further study of how infectious diseases occur, why they occur, how to prevent them, and how to manage them once they occur. In 1866, Dr. William Farr began collecting data on cholera deaths and studying the characteristics of persons who died from the disease. He found that living in crowded cities is detrimental to public health, and some urban environments are more dangerous than others, especially for children. Based on his studies, Farr recommended building a sewer system to separate waste from public drinking water to avoid epidemics. However, building a system was not a complete cure for infectious diseases, because bacteria could still contaminate drinking water in other ways. To further protect public health, scientists suggested adding a small amount of chlorine to kill bacteria that accidentally got into the water.

In 1854, Louis Pasteur began studying why beer and wine spoil. He found that heating prevented beer or wine from spoiling, and others applied the process, called pasteurization, to whole milk. Scientists found that pasteurization saves lives, so by 1920, the sale of unpasteurized milk was outlawed in America. Today, the Food and Drug Administration inspects and regulates food and pharmaceuticals that Americans consume. Beyond pasteurization, chlorination, and pharmaceutical regulation, another major advance that increased human longevity was the introduction of artificial fertilizers. Synthetic fertilizers and more efficient production of meat from chickens, pigs, and cattle, increased the amount of food available to feed the human population, which increased dramatically. In 1928, Alexander Fleming discovered penicillin, which killed bacteria and saved millions of lives. Another factor that increased the average life expectancy of humans were auto safety regulations. More people have died in car crashes than from all the wars fought by the United States since it was founded. To lower auto death rates, traffic lights were installed in 1914, speed limits were posted, and roads were designed to make them safer. In 1955, Ford introduced safety door latches, lap belts, a padded dashboard and sun visors, and a recessed steering wheel to their cars, but customer interest was low. In 1959, Swedish manufacturer Volvo introduced the first successful car safety device, a three-point seatbelt with lap and chest straps. Tests showed the three-point seatbelt reduced traffic mortality by 75 percent, resulting in the avoidance of many deaths in car crashes.

2

GENETICS, ENVIRONMENT, AND AGING

Longevity is affected by genetics, environment, and disease, but some individuals seem to defy aging and death. For example, researchers have found that individuals living in what are called Blue Zones live longer and are healthier than the general population. However, among rich Western countries, the incidence of illnesses such as heart disease or dementia reduces the quality of life among older citizens, so they don't enjoy their golden years. Scientists have found that genetic factors have a modest influence on how long a person can expect to live, (genes control at least 40 percent of the variation in human longevity), while diet, exercise, lifestyle, stress, smoking, and alcohol use control the remaining variation in human longevity. Access to good medical care, social relationships, diet, exercise, socioeconomic status, and education all influence how long a person can expect to live. Surveys of long-lived individuals find that they remain healthy for much of their lives and don't develop major diseases until old age. Scientists who study life expectancy believe the limit of human longevity is about 120 years, which is close to the age of the oldest known woman with a valid birth certificate, who lived to 122.

Studying how genetics and environment affect longevity requires special experimental designs. Scientists have found that studies using identical and fraternal twins separated at birth, or the resemblances of children to their biological and adoptive parents, produce the best estimates of heritability for longevity because these methodologies allow researchers to separate the effects of genes and environments. Other longevity researchers study populations where people generally live to 100 to identify factors that extend the human lifespan.

Twin and Family Studies. Studies have found that identical twins, who share 100 percent of their genes, are more similar in longevity than fraternal twins, who share only 50 percent of their genes, even when both sets of twins were separated soon after birth and raised in adoptive families. Moreover, children whose parents enjoy a long life can expect to live longer than the offspring of parents who die young, whether these children were reared by their biological parents or adopted into a different family. Studies of identical and fraternal twins separated at an early age and reared apart are useful when studying the effects of genetics and environment on behavior. Three sets of data are available containing identical and fraternal twins who were separated early in life and reared by adopted parents. Bouchard studied forty-four pairs of identical twins reared apart and twenty-five pairs of fraternal twins reared apart; Finnish researchers collected one hundred sixty-five pairs of twins reared apart; and Swedish investigators followed nine hundred sixty-one pairs of twins reared apart. Bouchard's study measured the IQs of twins who were separated soon after birth, so these data are not relevant to understanding the heritability of longevity. The Finnish Twin Study found that twins and singletons adopted at an early age and reared apart did not differ significantly in their average life expectancy. Moreover, the Swedish Adoptive Twin Study found that the influence of genetics on behavior is as strong later in life as during childhood, suggesting that longer intervals of environmental influences do not have a significant influence on longevity.

Adopted twin studies suggest that approximately 75 percent of the variation in longevity is controlled by genetics. In contrast, the remaining variation in life expectancy is influenced by environmental factors such as smoking, diet, stress, lifestyle, socioeconomic status, and disease. On average, women live approximately six years longer than men due to hormonal and immune system differences, and because women receive an XX sex chromosome, while men receive an XY sex chromosome, which allows more degenerative sex-linked genetic diseases to be expressed in men than women. The heritability of longevity is slightly higher among men (r = 0.26) than women (r = 0.23), and the heritability of living to be one hundred is estimated to be r= 0.48 among men and r = 0.33 for women. The children of centenarians are seven times more likely to live one hundred years compared with the average person whose parents died at an average age. Offspring of centenarians are also less likely to develop heart disease or prostate cancer than other individuals.

Since the genetics of longevity is based on multiple genes, it's unlikely that researchers will find many single genes that contribute significantly to living longer. To date, scientists have discovered that variations in the gene APOE (which participates in making a protein that helps transport cholesterol and other fats in the body) have a modest effect on longevity, suggesting that future research may discover a few other single gene determinants of living longer. People who live to one hundred share several traits, including not smoking, avoiding obesity, and dealing effectively with stress. As a result, they are unlikely to develop high blood pressure, heart disease, cancer, or Type 2 diabetes. An early study of gifted children by Lewis Terman explored associations between intelligence and longevity.

Terman's Gifted Children. In 1921, Lewis Terman, who developed the Stanford-Binet Intelligence Test, began studying over one thousand five hundred gifted children in the San Francisco area. His goal was to examine the characteristics and behaviors of these bright children and see if he could discover the origins of intellectual leadership. Decades later, other psychologists contacted these gifted individuals when they were adults, to discover why some had lived long healthy lives while others died early. These later scientists wanted to study the characteristics of adults in the Terman sample who lived a long time. Their first task was to record how long each Terman subject lived and their specific cause of death. Next, these psychologists studied the Terman participants' personal traits such as persistence, happiness, attitude toward life, education, parental divorce, exercise habits, careers, religious beliefs, and social connections. The psychologists studying Terman's gifted children as adults found that several behavioral traits are associated with living longer. For example, they discovered that among the Terman subjects, prudent, dependable, persistent, and well-organized people lived longer than their risk-taking disorganized peers.

The scientists who studied Terman's subjects concluded that conscientious adults lived longer because they had more stable marriages, stronger social relationships, less stressful careers, and avoided accidents because they were more careful than their risk-taking peers. These psychologists also found that individuals who scored low in conscientiousness were likely to die young, while adults who scored in the middle range on conscientiousness died in middle age, and adults who scored high in conscientiousness lived the longest. These scientists also found that individuals low in conscientiousness were more likely to suffer from one or more chronic diseases compared with individuals who were high in conscientiousness. The psychologists studying Terman's subjects also found that cheerful people died at an earlier age than more serious ones and concluded that happy individuals engaged in risky behaviors which cause accidents and early death. They believed that optimistic individuals are not so aware of threats, and as a result, they die at an early age compared with pessimistic persons who pay more attention to dangers in their environment.

These scientists also found that having social connections, living in a loving family, dealing effectively with stress, having an interesting career, enjoying a stable marriage, avoiding being overweight, drinking moderately, not smoking, and being physically active increased longevity among Terman's subjects. The researchers concluded that if individuals want to live longer, they should avoid anxiety, depression, thoughts of suicide, using dangerous drugs, and driving fast. For men, having a stable marriage was essential to longevity, but that was not true for women. Females in the Terman study were able to substitute other social relationships for a failed marriage.

These psychologists also found that individuals who attend church live longer than agnostics, suggesting that prayer and meditation may lead to a longer life. Finally, longer lived individuals had goals that keep them engaged and satisfied, while those individuals in the Terman study who had no long-term goals died at a younger age. Smoking, ingesting heavy metals, being exposed to pesticides, breathing polluted air, or drinking contaminated water shortened life expectancy. Additionally, exposure to radon, X-rays, or nuclear waste, and infections from viruses, molds, or bacteria were associated with early death. Finally, having an auto accident or falling were associated with dying early. Another method of studying genetics, environment, and longevity is to compare individuals who live in what are called Blue Zones (where a significant portion of the population lives to one hundred) with groups who live in areas where people die at a normal age.

Blue Zones. People who reside in Blue Zones often live to be one hundred, compared with average Americans who live about seventy-seven years on average. Scientists have discovered five Blue Zones where individuals live long and healthy lives. Using epidemiological data, birth certificates, and statistical analyses, Blue Zones were found in Sardinia, Italy; Okinawa, Japan; Loma Linda, California among Seventh-day Adventists; Ikaria, Greece; and Nicoya, Costa Rica. Individuals in these five zones survive to one hundred at ten times the rate found in other populations. Factors associated with living longer and healthier lives in these Blue Zones include exercise, having a purpose in life, minimizing stress, avoiding being overweight, eating a healthy diet, drinking alcohol in moderation, having close family connections, and finding friends who practice and support healthy lifestyles. Long-lived people don't have to force themselves to eat right or exercise, because healthy routines are part of their natural lifestyles. Individuals in Blue Zones have jobs that require them to exercise naturally by walking, planting, harvesting, and managing a household without using mechanical conveniences. They also eat mostly grains, fruits, and vegetables from their fields and develop close connections with neighbors.

Moreover, individuals in these Blue Zones have a sense of purpose in their lives, so they wake up each morning with a plan for the day. Blue Zone inhabitants experience problems like everyone else, but they take time every day to think about their ancestors, pray, take a nap, or engage in a happy hour to manage their stress. Long-lived individuals in Blue

Zones avoid obesity by stopping eating when they are 80 percent full, consume their smallest meal in the evening, don't snack between meals, and eat a diet high in fish, fruits, vegetables, whole grains, and nuts. Residents of Blue Zones eat a plant-rich diet and consume red meat only four or five times a month. They drink alcohol in moderation, having no more than one or two glasses of wine daily.

Individuals in Blue Zones engage in some faith-based service on a weekly basis and put their families first. They also take care of their aging parents in their own homes, invest time, money, and effort in their children, and generally stay faithful to a single partner their entire life. Finally, long-lived individuals in Blue Zones live in communities that practice and support healthy lifestyles such as not smoking, drinking in moderation, exercising, avoiding obesity, and associating with family and friends. What are the specific characteristics of people in each Blue Zone?

Sardinia. Sardinia is an island off the coast of Italy and is home to the longest-lived men in the world. They herd sheep in mountainous terrain and walk an average of five miles daily up and down hills, following their flocks. Natural exercise promotes heart health and avoids stress to bones, muscles, and tendons that occur when running a marathon. The Sardinian diet contains whole-grains, beans, vegetables, and fruits. These individuals eat meat only on Sunday, and they drink moderate quantities of wine daily.

Okinawa. Okinawa is an island south of Japan and is home to the longest-lived women in the world. They form close-knit social networks at age five and know they will be cared for by their friends no matter what happens in their life. The average age of Okinawan women is one hundred two years. They gather to drink sake and gossip with friends daily, don't overeat, and devote themselves to their families.

Adventist Community. Members of the Adventist community in Loma Linda, California, live ten years longer, on average, than the typical American. Their diet is taken from the Bible, and consists primarily of vegetables, nuts, and legumes. They never work on the Sabbath and say active well into their nineties.

Nicoya, Costa Rica. People in Nicoya, Costa Rica, spend less than 20 percent as much as Americans on health care but are twice as likely to live to ninety years. Costa Ricans devote their lives to family, eat no processed food, and enjoy a diet rich in tropical fruits. They drink water rich in calcium and magnesium, promoting strong bones and healthy hearts.

Ikaria, Greece. Residents of Ikaria, Greece, a small island in the Aegean Sea, live eight years longer on average than Americans. They experience little cancer, have low rates of heart disease, and rarely develop dementia. People living in Ikaria eat a diet consisting of fruits, vegetables, whole grains, beans, potatoes, and olive oil. They take naps daily and enjoy life. Studying Blue Zone individuals allowed scientists to discover what constitutes a healthy lifestyle, how to live longer, and remain happy. However, genetic diseases decrease life expectancy.

Genetic Diseases. Some genetic diseases run in families and may be passed from one or both parents to their children. The six most common heritable genetic diseases that shorten life expectancy are sickle cell anemia, cystic fibrosis, Tay-Sachs disease, hemophilia, Huntington's disease, and muscular dystrophy. Sickle cell anemia is caused by defective genes that control the production of hemoglobin proteins.

Individuals who suffer from sickle cell anemia produce blood cells that are rigid and shaped like a sickle.

Sickle Cell Disease. Sickle cell disease is the most common inherited blood disorder in the United States, affecting approximately one hundred thousand Americans, mostly of African ancestry. Children in this afflicted group have a 75 percent chance of being born with the disorder if both parents carry the defective gene. However, if a child inherits only one copy of the defective gene for sickle cell anemia, his or her blood will be normal. Red blood cells are usually round and flexible, but sickle cells are rigid and misshapen, so they often slow or block the flow of blood in vessels. A major symptom of sickle cell disease is anemia caused by deformed blood cells dying more quickly than normal blood cells, creating a shortage of cells to carry oxygen to the body, producing shortness of breath and fatigue. Another symptom of sickle cell disease is recurring pain caused by sickle cells blocking the flow of blood in small arteries and veins. The pain varies in severity and can last for hours or days. Some people with sickle cell disease experience a few episodes of pain per year while others may experience a dozen or more pain episodes annually. This genetic disorder can also cause swelling of hands and feet, and some affected individuals experience frequent infections because their spleen has been damaged by defective sickle cells. Sickle cell disease can also cause problems with vision because vessels in the eye become blocked with sickle cells and damage the retina. Other symptoms of sickle cell disease include paralysis of one side of the body, mental confusion, difficulty walking, sudden changes in vision, numbness of limbs, and severe headaches.

Another common genetic disease is cystic fibrosis.

<u>Cystic Fibrosis</u>. This disorder affects the body's production of mucus, sweat, and digestive juices. Cystic fibrosis is caused by a defective gene that interferes with the production of proteins that regulate the movement of salt and water in and out of cells. People who suffer from cystic fibrosis produce thick, sticky mucus that may damage their respiratory, digestive, and reproductive systems. This genetic disorder is most

common among Northern Europeans. Historically, individuals suffering from cystic fibrosis experienced chronic degeneration of the lungs, digestive system, and other organs, but with modern medical care, these patients can live a nearly normal life for around fifty years (which is still nearly thirty years less than the average life expectancy of Americans). Today, cystic fibrosis can be diagnosed at an early age before serious symptoms develop if physicians order the proper tests. If the disorder does not develop until later, the adult symptoms are usually milder than when the illness develops early in life. Symptoms of cystic fibrosis include a recurring cough, wheezing, limited energy, frequent lung infections, stuffy nose, and repeated sinus infections. Other symptoms of cystic fibrosis are caused by blocking of ducts from the pancreas to the small intestine, producing poor weight gain, slow growth, blocked intestines in some newborns, and chronic constipation. Individuals suffering from cystic fibrosis need constant medical care to survive. Complications of cystic fibrosis include damaged lungs, frequent infections, coughing of blood, respiratory failure, poor nutrition, diabetes, liver disease, infertility in men, lowered fertility among women, porous bones, anxiety or depression, and intestinal cancers. Tay-Sachs disease is another inherited disorder that's fatal among affected individuals.

Tay-Sachs Disease. This generic disorder is most frequent among Eastern European Jews, French Canadian communities in Quebec, and within the Cajun communities of Louisiana. Tay-Sachs disease is caused by a lack of an enzyme that breaks down fats, allowing fatty substances to reach toxic levels in the brains of affected individuals. Most often, symptoms of Tay-Sachs disease appear around six months of age in affected infants. Over time, these children suffer seizures, vision and hearing loss, and paralysis. Children who inherit Tay-Sachs disease usually live only a few years. A juvenile form of Tay-Sachs disease can appear later in childhood, and these individuals may survive into their teens. Symptoms of infantile Tay-Sachs disease include red spots in the eyes, loss of motor coordination, muscle weakness, seizures, loss of vision and hearing, poor mental functioning, and macrocephaly (abnormal growth of the head). The Juvenile form of Tay-Sachs disease causes behavior problems, gradual loss of motor control, recurring respiratory infections, loss of vision and hearing, decline of mental abilities, and stiffness in muscles and joints. The adult form of Tay-Sachs disease is characterized by muscle weakness, tremors, loss of the ability to walk, problems speaking, and psychiatric disorders. Another inherited disease is hemophilia, which causes excessive bleeding.

Hemophilia. This genetic disorder is more common among males than females and is caused by a deficiency in blood-clotting agents, producing excessive internal bleeding among affected individuals. The gene that causes hemophilia is on the X chromosome, which encodes gender. Since males inherit only one X chromosome from their mother, if she is a carrier of hemophilia, her male children have a high risk of being affected by the disease. Because newborn females inherit two copies of the X chromosome, they have a much smaller chance of developing hemophilia (females must inherit the defective gene from both parents to be affected). Minor cuts or abrasions of the skin are not usually serious problems for individuals suffering from hemophilia, but internal bleeding, especially in the brain, can be life-threatening. Early treatments involved replacing blood-clotting factors through transfusions, but newer treatments don't require frequent transfusions. Symptoms of hemophilia include excessive internal bleeding, frequent bruising, recurring pain, swelling and stiffness of joints, blood in the urine or stool, and recurring nose bleeds.

The most serious complication is bleeding in the brain caused by a minor bump to the head. In normal individuals, proteins in the blood form clots and stop bleeding, but if these clotting proteins are missing, as happens among individuals who suffer from hemophilia, excessive internal bleeding can occur and may be fatal. Hemophilia is usually inherited, but a few individuals may develop the disorder during pregnancy, from autoimmune reactions when they develop cancer or because of an adverse drug reaction. Other serious complications of hemophilia are pain in joints, recurring infections, and adverse reactions to clotting factor treatments. Another inherited disorder is Huntington's disease, a life-threatening illness that appears in mid-life among individuals who inherit the defective gene.

Huntington's Disease. This inherited disorder causes progressive destruction of nerve cells in the brain, producing mental deterioration and loss of muscle function. Drugs are available to manage the disorder, but they do not prevent the decline of physical and mental abilities. The primary symptoms of this disease are movement problems, mental health issues, and difficulty planning. The disorder can cause muscle rigidity, jerking movements, unusual eye movements, and difficulty walking, speaking, or swallowing. People suffering from Huntington's disease usually can't work or live independently. The disorder causes cognitive disabilities, difficulties thinking, rigid thought patterns, lack of impulse control, poor self-awareness, difficulty producing words, and trouble learning new information. Common mental health symptoms include irritability, depression, apathy, withdrawal, fatigue, and recurring thoughts of suicide. Some individuals with Huntington's disease suffer from obsessive-compulsive behaviors, elevated mood, or bipolar disorder. Younger individuals with Huntington's disease have difficulty paying attention and may be aggressive or disruptive in class. Another inherited disease impedes motor development.

Muscular Dystrophy. This genetic disease interferes with the production of proteins necessary for healthy muscle development. Muscular dystrophy occurs most often among boys and symptoms usually appear during childhood. There is no cure, but drugs can manage serious symptoms for a few years. The main effect of muscular dystrophy is progressive muscle weakness, which can lead to falls, difficulty sitting, and difficulty running, and often causes affected individuals to walk on their toes. These patients also experience learning problems, delayed physical growth, and muscle pain or stiffness. Muscular dystrophy occurs in both sexes and can appear at any age, but most often appears among young boys, and they have a higher risk of passing the disease to their children. Complications include difficulty learning to walk, inability to use the arms, problems breathing, curved spine, heart problems, and difficulty swallowing.

Summary. Aging is controlled by genetics, environment, and disease, but people living in what are called Blue Zones live longer and are healthier than the general population. Scientists estimate that genetic factors account for about 40 percent of the variation in human longevity, while diet, exercise, lifestyle, stress, smoking, and alcohol consumption account for the rest. Good medical care, social connections, a healthy diet, exercise, high socioeconomic status, and education also influence how long a person can expect to live. Studies using adopted identical and fraternal twins separated at birth or the resemblances of children to their biological and adoptive parents produce good estimates of heritability for longevity. The heritability of longevity is higher among men (r = 0.26) than women (r = 0.23), and the heritability of living to be one hundred is estimated to be r= 0.48 among men and r = 0.33 for women. The children of centenarians are seven times more likely to live one hundred years compared with the average person whose parents died at a normal age.

Psychologists studying Terman's gifted children found that cheerful people die at an earlier age than more serious ones They also found that having social connections, living in a loving family, dealing effectively with stress, having an interesting career, enjoying a stable marriage, avoiding being overweight, drinking moderately, not smoking, and being physically active increase longevity. These scientists also showed that men in a stable marriage live longer, but that was not true for women. Females seem able to substitute other social relationships for a failed marriage and suffer no ill effects as a result. These psychologists also found that individuals who attend church live longer than agnostics, suggesting that prayer and meditation may lead to a longer life. Long lived individuals have goals that keep them engaged and satisfied, while those individuals in the Terman study who had no long-term goals died young.

Smoking, exposure to pesticides, polluted air, and drinking contaminated water shortened life expectancy. Additionally, exposure to radon, nuclear waste, and infections cause early death. Finally, auto accidents and falling are associated with dying early. Another method of studying genetics, environment, and longevity is to compare individuals who live in what are called Blue Zones.

Scientists have discovered Blue Zones in Sardinia, Italy; Okinawa, Japan; Loma Linda, California among Seventh-day Adventists; Ikaria, Greece; and Nicoya, Costa Rica. Individuals in these five zones survive to one hundred at ten times the rate found in other populations. Factors associated with living longer and healthier lives in these Blue Zones include exercise, having a purpose in life, minimizing stress, avoiding being overweight, eating a healthy plant-based diet, drinking alcohol in moderation, having close family connections, and friends who practice and support healthy lifestyles. Long-lived people don't have to force themselves to eat right or exercise, because healthy routines are part of their natural lifestyle. However, genetic diseases decrease life expectancy, even among individuals in blue zones.

The most common heritable genetic diseases that shorten life expectancy are sickle cell anemia, cystic fibrosis, Tay-Sachs disease, hemophilia, Huntington's disease, and muscular dystrophy. Sickle cell anemia is caused by defective genes that control the production of hemoglobin proteins, and individuals with sickle cell disease produce blood cells that are rigid and shaped like a sickle. Another common genetic disease is cystic fibrosis, which is caused by a defective gene that interferes with the movement of salt and water into and out of cells. People with cystic fibrosis produce thick, sticky mucus that can damage their respiratory, digestive, and reproductive systems. This genetic disorder is most common among Northern Europeans.

Tay-Sachs disease is an inherited disorder that's fatal among affected individuals and is most frequent among Eastern European Jews, French Canadian communities in Quebec, and within the Cajun communities of Louisiana. Tay-Sachs disease is caused by the lack of an enzyme that digests fats, allowing fatty substances to reach toxic levels in the brains of affected individuals.

Hemophilia causes excessive bleeding. This genetic disorder is more common among males than females and is caused by a deficiency in blood-clotting agents, producing excessive internal bleeding among affected individuals. Symptoms of hemophilia include excessive internal bleeding, frequent bruising, recurring pain, swelling and stiffness of joints, blood in the urine or stool, and recurring nose bleeds. Huntington's disease is a life-threatening illness that appears in mid-life among individuals who inherit the defective gene. This disorder causes progressive destruction of nerve cells, producing mental deterioration and loss of muscle function. Major symptoms include mental health issues, difficulty planning, muscle rigidity, jerking movements, unusual eye movements, and difficulty walking, speaking, or swallowing. Muscular dystrophy occurs most often among boys and symptoms usually appear during childhood. There is no cure, but drugs can manage serious symptoms for a few years. The main symptom of muscular dystrophy is progressive muscle weakness, which can produce falling, problems sitting, difficulty running, and often causes affected individuals to walk on their toes.

3

THE SCIENCE OF LIVING LONGER

Most people want to live a long, healthy life. However, can physicians make practical recommendations about how to live a long, healthy life, and do they know how to slow or reverse aging? The answer is a qualified yes. Genetics has a modest influence on longevity, but lifestyle makes a huge difference in whether a person lives a long healthy life. Among lower animals, genes can make a big difference in life expectancy. For example, scientists have found that changing a single gene in a worm can double its lifespan. Specifically, they found a gene called def-2 associated with worms living much longer. Scientists began to understand genetics and longevity when they initiated the Human Genome Project, which has produced a complete map of the human genome. This research allows scientists to study how single genes are related to human longevity. Moreover, discovery of the gene editing tool CRISPR has raised the possibility that scientists may eventually learn how to alter human genes to achieve better health and longer lives, although early attempts have shown there can be unintended consequences associated with altering a human genome. Researchers use several methods to study human longevity.

Scientists study human longevity using methods developed in the fields of demography, population genetics, molecular biology, psychology, cell metabolism, nutrition, and pharmacology. There are several reasons humans age, and some individuals live longer than others, including genetics, diet, exercise, social connections, work, and income. Humans have been interested in living longer for centuries, but they don't want to live a life filled with chronic disease and pain. Modern medicine offers procedures that claim to increase life expectancy, but how can individuals distinguish truth from medical hype? Understanding what factors can increase longevity is difficult, but there are confirmed benefits associated with regular exercise and eating a healthy diet. In the last century, the average life expectancy of men increased from forty-eight to seventy-four years, and the average life expectancy of women increased from fifty-one to eighty years. However, most of the increase in average life expectancy occurred because of reduced child mortality, rather than by extending the lifespan of the average adult. Adult life expectancy has increased by a factor of approximately two, while the average expected age of infants has increased by a factor of ten. Scientists have tried to define what they mean by aging so they can study longevity, but there are several theories about what causes aging, and scientists disagree about how and why humans age.

Theories of Aging. Most theories of aging assume that after reproduction, there has been little evolutionary pressure to extend life, which is why people age and die. Aging begins around forty for the average human, although there is wide individual variation in when aging begins and how quickly it progresses. Human longevity is associated with declines in the functioning of stem cells, so some scientists have speculated that if they could find a way to maintain the viability of stem cells, humans could live a long healthy life. During early development, the human body creates new organs from stem cells, so scientists have wondered if it might be possible to program embryonic stem cells to repair the older human body and slow or even halt aging. Biologists have also suggested that aging occurs because the human body accumulates mutations, caused by random damage to genes. Evolutionary biologists believe living a long time was not adaptive for humans, because after adults reproduce, there is no evolutionary advantage to living beyond the time required to rear offspring. Also, because women are the main caregivers, they have evolved to live longer than men. Another theory of aging assumes that free radicals accumulate in the human body, and cause aging.

The Nobel chemist Linus Pauling suggested that antioxidants might slow or stop the accumulation of free radicals and allow people to live longer. In an attempt to prolong his own life, Pauling consumed huge quantities of vitamin C. He lived to age ninety-three, so perhaps his theory was valid, but a sample of one is too small to support a reliable conclusion. However, research has shown that regular aerobic exercise increases longevity, even if these individuals don't consume large quantities of vitamin C. Paradoxically, experiencing stress early in life extends the lifespan of animals, while prolonged stress later in life decreases longevity. Another theory of ageing is that humans are programmed to die at a certain age after they have reproduced and reared their offspring. This theory seems to apply to salmon, who leave the ocean, swim upstream to where they spawned, reproduce, and then die. Another theory of aging is that toxic environmental factors damage DNA, and these mutations decrease longevity. This theory is supported by studies showing genetic defects can cause lethal diseases. In addition to speculating about what causes aging, biologists have also considered ways to help humans live longer.

How to Increase Longevity. Scientists have suggested that it may be possible to increase the human lifespan by replacing old cells with new ones. Since stem cells are the primary source of new cells, differences in their regenerative abilities may contribute to variation in longevity among individuals. If scientists could understand why some humans live longer than others, it might be possible to extend the average life expectancy. Different genes and cells regulate the growth and maintenance of the human body, and these might hold the key to increased longevity.

For example, germ cells produce a new individual when a sperm and ova unite, implant, and grow. Also, embryonic stem cells can grow into different adult cells. However, adult stem cells lose this plasticity and can produce only a few types of cells, and biologists don't understand why this happens. If scientists could understand what causes the transformation from embryonic to adult stem cells, they might discover the key to living a long healthy life. In addition to considering stem cells as possible keys to increased human longevity, scientists have also found that caps at the ends of chromosomes protect them from environmental damage, and these caps become shorter as humans age, suggesting they may be involved in controlling longevity. Biologists have suggested that the shortening of chromosome end caps may be the cause of aging because having short caps is associated with cell disfunction.

At one time, physicians believed blood transfusions would rejuvenate the human body, but that hypothesis has been disproved. Biologists have also noted that some species live longer than others and have studied these variations to understand why animals age. Also, life expectancy is different among various human groups, and this fact may offer clues to the causes of aging. For example, Black American men experience higher mortality rates from heart disease, diabetes, and high blood pressure than other ethnic groups, which reduces their average life expectancy to seventy years. That is four years less than the average lifespan of white men in America. Life expectancy in the United States is also associated with income, so wealthier individuals live longer on average than their poor peers. Physicians know that not smoking, avoiding obesity, and managing stress effectively increase longevity. On average, women live six years longer than men in the United States, and that difference may also offer clues to what causes aging. The major risk of early death among women is maternal mortality, especially for young and older females. Paradoxically, the likelihood of dying decreases after humans reach old age. The major factors that allow Americans to live longer are exercise, vaccines, improved nutrition, antibiotics, and effective treatments for chronic illnesses. However, there seems to be a limit to how long humans can live. The longest-lived woman who had a valid birth certificate died at age one hundred twenty-two, and the longest-lived man with a valid birth certificate died at one hundred sixteen. Some scientists have asked if it's a good idea to extend human life because of overpopulation.

Is Longevity Research Ethical? Some critics have suggested that scientists should not study human longevity to extend the human lifespan because the world faces overpopulation, and allowing humans to live longer would make the problem worse. Is that a valid concern? Is it ethical to study aging when humanity may be facing overpopulation, famine, and disaster in a few generations? Scientists believe studying aging is not a problem because older individuals cannot reproduce so they will not increase the total human population. Moreover, the goal of longevity research is to extend the life of individuals and keep them healthy, not simply to allow people to live longer while suffering from chronic diseases. However, if scientists are successful in extending life and maintaining their health, governments may need to change the rules associated with Social Security and Medicare, because living longer will increase the costs to these programs. Most scientists believe that's a minor problem compared with the benefits of living a long healthy life. Individuals who live longer will likely work more, pay taxes for additional years, and produce a net benefit to society. Scientists know that lifestyle changes can help individuals live longer. To enjoy additional healthy years, individuals should eat a diet containing fruits, vegetables, whole grains, fish, and low-fat dairy products. Additionally, individuals who want to live a long healthy life should avoid eating processed foods high in sugar and salt, smoking, and becoming overweight, sleep about eight hours every night, exercise daily, schedule an annual physical exam, get proper medical care, and learn to deal with stress.

Achieving and maintaining a healthy lifestyle is difficult for many people, so medical science is trying to develop a pill that would help individuals live longer. Is that even possible? To know whether science can develop an aging treatment, we need to understand what factors are associated with longevity. One promising line of research is studying animals that live long and healthy lives.

Long-Lived Animals. There is enormous variation in the lifespans of different species, and most long-lived creatures live in the sea. For example, the Greenland shark is believed to live around five hundred years. Also, large animals generally live longer than small ones. However, within a species, the opposite is true. Small dogs live longer than large ones. To assess this phenomenon, biologists created the longevity quotient (LQ) to measure how close an animal's lifespan to is its expected longevity based on size. An LQ of one means an animal species has the lifespan expected for its size, while animals that live longer than expected based on their size earn LQs larger than one. An LQ below one means the species lives fewer years than would be expected based on its size. Brown bats have an LQ of ten, meaning they live much longer than would be expected based on their size. Another way to study longevity is to take advantage of the fact that genes which increase lifespan in one species often appear in others, so it might be possible to transfer longevity genes from long-lived species into the human genome and increase people's lifespan. If scientists could transfer longevity genes from long-lived animals, such as whales and naked mole rats to humans, people might live longer. The goal of longevity research is not simply to extend life, but to allow humans to live a life free from chronic disease. Increased longevity would be a curse if it produced unhealthy individuals who live a long time. Consequently, scientists are interested in extending both the number of years a person lives, and the quality of these extra years. To do that, biologists need to understand what causes aging and develop accurate ways to measure it.

Measuring Aging. Aging can be assessed by looking at cognition, memory, balance, strength, freedom from pain, and the incidence of illness. Individuals who live longer appear to be naturally healthy and have few age-related diseases, so they experience a long natural healthy life. Scientists have begun to study individuals who live a long healthy life, hoping to discover clues to increasing human longevity. Surprisingly, most individuals can accurately assess who is likely to live a long healthy life. For example, if people are asked to estimate how long they think another individual is likely to live (this estimate is called a person's perceived age), physicians have found these estimates are correlated with actual age at death. Moreover, an individual's estimated wealth is also correlated with how long he or she lives. Scientists have found that eating a restricted diet increases human lifespan, but is that a healthy way to increase longevity?

Dietary Restriction and Longevity. Throughout history, humans have been subjected to restricted diets during war or crop failures. For example, calories were restricted in Denmark during the First World War, and in Norway during the Second World War. Later studies showed that individuals who lived on a restricted diet lived 30 percent longer than people who enjoyed a normal diet. Scientists have also found that food-deprived rats live longer than animals fed a normal diet. However, dietary restriction is associated with slower brain functioning and poor memory, so trying to live longer by eating a restricted diet is a mixed blessing. Studies show that intermittent fasting can increase longevity and slow the development of cancers in animals.

Alternating normal eating with fasting also improves tissue regeneration and boosts cognitive functioning. However, living on a restricted diet causes muscle loss in human adults. This loss occurs naturally with age, producing a risk of falls, broken bones, and death among older adults. Muscle loss is associated with changes in mitochondria, which regulate energy production in cells. Loss of mitochondrial function is also associated with the development of Parkinson's disease, Alzheimer's, and Amyotrophic Lateral Sclerosis (ALS or Lou Gehrig's Disease). Having children also affects human longevity.

Reproduction and Aging. It has been known for centuries that women often develop reproductive problems in their late thirties. This biological clock limits the time human females can produce healthy children. Reproductive decline among women is one of the earliest signs of aging. Men also suffer reproductive decline with age, but at a much slower rate than women. However, scientists have found that women who produce healthy children after age forty are four times more likely to live to one hundred compared with women who don't produce children after age forty. This finding suggests that for females, being able to reproduce later in life is a sign of slow aging. Physicians have also found that a woman's ability to reproduce is regulated by the quality of her ova rather than the absolute number she possesses. Once women enter menopause, they tend to age faster, but this accelerated aging can be slowed with supplemental hormone treatments. What factors control aging in women and why do they life longer than men?

Why Women Live Longer. Females live longer than males in most species, but the reasons are complex. Natural selection would increase the lifespan of women if living longer enhances their reproductive success, so evolutionary pressures may explain why women live longer than men. Also, women who can reproduce at an advanced age would have a reproductive advantage, because when food is scarce, they could postpone reproduction and become pregnant when the food supply recovers. Another theory of why women live longer than men is that grandmothers who live longer confer extra fitness on their family genes because they help raise their grandchildren, improving the family's genetic fitness. The problem with this theory is that female worms, who do not invest energy in raising their offspring, also live longer than male worms, although there may be another explanation for that effect.

Another reason women may live longer than men is because human females invest more time and energy in raising their children than men.

Biologists believe women live longer than men because they make a larger reproductive investment in their offspring compared with males, and therefore females who live longer are more likely to raise their offspring to reproductive age, contributing to family genetic fitness. Another theory of why women live longer than men is because of sexual interactions between males and females. Perhaps women live longer than men because they enjoy sex and produce more children, contributing to their family fitness. Average human lifespan has increased over the last three hundred years, but women have enjoyed a larger increase than men. It may be that healthy women are more sexually active, and that's why they live longer. Also, women who have longer chromosome caps (the protective telomeres that are located at the ends of chromosomes) are more likely to live in a committed relationship and have sex at least once a week compared with females who have shorter chromosome caps. Moreover, people with better immune systems are healthier and have sex more often than individuals with weaker immune systems (probably because individuals with weak immune systems are more often ill). Finally, women who enter menopause before forty have decreased sex drive, experience less sexual satisfaction, and die earlier than women who experience menopause at a normal age.

Biologists have also suggested that human females live longer than males because their metabolic rate is lower. Researchers also believe that the X chromosomes of women may explain why they live longer, because some alleles on the X chromosome of older women are not turned off as they are among younger women and that may enhance older females' health. Men benefit reproductively by living longer and enjoying multiple matings, while females, because they spend more time nurturing offspring, may experience higher mortality rates if they produce many children because giving birth can be dangerous. Physicians believe that most studies showing a correlation between sexual satisfaction and longevity are the result of better general health, a more effective immune system, or genetic differences. Other factors that cause women to live longer than men is that human males develop cardiovascular diseases more often than women. However, because women live longer than men, they are more likely to develop Alzheimer's disease. Because women live longer, four out of five people who live to one hundred, and the ten longest lived humans in history were all women. Among all species, females live longer than males in about 60 percent of cases. For example, among nonhuman primates such as orangutans, gorillas, and chimpanzees, females live significantly longer than males, but among horses, bats, and rabbits, males live longer than females. Social factors also influence the longevity of males and females differently.

Social Relations and Longevity. Being married increases the longevity of men by almost two years but *decreases* the lifespan of women by more than a year.

Scientists believe the differences in longevity between married men and women are caused by the higher stress associated with being married for women. However, if a wife is much younger than her husband, her longevity is not affected by being married. That may explain why women marry older men. On the other hand, perhaps women are more resistant to stress when they are young. Studies also show that human male promiscuity decreases longevity. Historical research comparing Chinese emperors who had normal sex lives with those who were promiscuous found that non-promiscuous emperors lived an average of eighteen years longer than their promiscuous peers. This result would happen by chance less than one time in one thousand, so the difference was highly significant. Scientists are not certain why being promiscuous shortened life expectancy among Chinese emperors, but it may have to do with being exposed to sexually transmitted diseases by having many sexual partners, or the result of other risky behaviors associated with promiscuity, such as other jealous males. Studies also show that understanding and reacting accurately to the environment increases the chance of survival.

Cognition and Aging. Memory loss is an early sign of decline among humans. Being able to remember is essential to survival, because people with memory loss are no longer able to adapt effectively to their environment. Memory loss is one of the worst effects of aging, and with increasing longevity, the incidence of cognitive decline is growing. Much of what we know about aging and cognitive decline is based on studies of Alzheimer's disease, and these data offer interesting insights about how to slow cognitive decline. Human neurons seem to decline randomly rather than in a systematic fashion. At the cellular level, metabolic processes that support neuron functioning fail in a random fashion and the cell deteriorates. This type of degeneration happens in all cells, but neurons, because they have synapses (the specialized structures that communicate among neurons) appear to deteriorate randomly over time in contrast to other cells, which decline as they mature. Synapses need a steady supply of new proteins, and neurotransmitters to function, so losing one of these essential elements can cause the synapse to die, producing cognitive decline. The first sign of neuronal aging is damage to the small vessels surrounding neural cells. Diabetes, high blood pressure, and strokes are major causes of damaged neurons. By avoiding vascular problems, humans can live longer and slow cognitive decline. Exercise and a healthy diet support vascular functioning, and sleep is essential to normal cognitive functioning. Scientists have found that giving older mice blood plasma from young mice enhances their ability to learn and recall. However, physicians believe normal aging and developing Alzheimer's disease are different processes so a cure for this disease would not stop aging.

Alzheimer's Disease. Cognitive decline occurs among most older individuals even if they don't develop the amyloid protein plaques associated with Alzheimer's disease. In addition to Alzheimer's disease, there are three other cognitive disorders associated with the accumulation of proteins in the brain. These are amyotrophic lateral sclerosis (ALS or

Lou Gehrig's Disease), Huntington's disease, and Parkinson's disease. These disorders are more likely to develop among older adults but are caused by processes distinct from the cognitive decline associated with aging. Neural inflammation and infections are associated with developing Alzheimer's. Moreover, genetic factors and poor cardiovascular health increase the chance of developing Alzheimer's, and there is no cure for this disorder. Treatments for Alzheimer's disease only mitigate the symptoms. Slowing the breakdown of acetylcholine can extend the cognitive abilities of patients suffering from Alzheimer's and allow them to function independently for a longer interval before requiring care. However, no treatment of Alzheimer's is a cure.

Some physicians have suggested that if treatments were begun earlier, they might be more effective, but at present, there is no way to detect Alzheimer's disease before it develops and by then it is generally too late. Blood tests, cognitive examinations, brain scans, and genetic markers have all been explored as ways to measure susceptibility to Alzheimer's disease, but none has been accurate. Black and Hispanic Americans are more likely to develop Alzheimer's disease compared with white Americans. Among individuals over eighty-five, 30 percent of whites develop the disease, while 60 percent of Black and Hispanic Americans are diagnosed with Alzheimer's at that age. This may happen because Black and Hispanic Americans are more likely to develop diabetes and high blood pressure, which are associated with cognitive decline as people age. If you want to slow aging, eat less and exercise regularly. However, many people find it difficult to limit weight gain and exercise every day, so they would like to have a drug that would help them live longer.

Intermittent dieting may increase longevity, but most people would rather take a pill than run five miles or go on a diet if they could enjoy the same health benefit. Another approach to extending lifespan is replacing cells lost during aging. Embryonic stem cells offer the possibility of living longer because they retain the ability to generate new cells. During the 1990s, gene therapy was believed to hold the key to living longer, but more recent studies show there are unintended consequences associated with gene editing and modern genetic scientists are no longer confident gene therapy will increase longevity.

Summary. Genetics has a modest influence on longevity, but lifestyle makes a huge difference in whether a person lives a long, healthy life. In the last century, the average life expectancy of men increased from 48 to 74 years, and that of women from 51 to 80 years. Most of this increase occurred because of reduced child mortality. Most theories of aging assume that after humans have reproduced, there has been little evolutionary pressure to extend life, and that's why people age and die. Aging begins around forty, but there is wide individual variation in when aging begins and how quickly it progresses. Longevity is associated with declines in stem cell functioning, random damage to genes, the accumulation of free radicals in the human body, and the fact that humans may be programmed to die at a certain age after they have reproduced. Scientists believe it may be possible to increase the human lifespan by replacing old cells with new ones. Another way to increase longevity might be to lengthen chromosome end caps because having short caps is associated with cell disfunction. Life expectancy is different among human groups, and this fact may offer clues to the causes of aging.

There is probably a limit to how long humans can live. The longest-lived woman who had a valid birth certificate died at age one hundred twenty-two, and the longest-lived man with a valid birth certificate died at one hundred sixteen. In the past, humans have been subjected to restricted diets during war or after crop failures and they lived longer than people who ate a normal diet. However, dietary restriction is associated with slower brain functioning and poor memory, so trying to live longer by eating a restricted diet probably won't work. Intermittent fasting can increase longevity and slow the development of cancers, because alternating normal eating with fasting seems to improve tissue regeneration and cognitive functioning. Women experience reproductive difficulties in their thirties, and this is a sign of aging. Men suffer reproductive decline at a much slower rate than women. Women who produce healthy children after age forty are four times more likely to live to be one hundred compared with women don't produce children after forty. One reason women live longer than men may be that those who can reproduce at an advanced age have a reproductive advantage when food is scarce, because they can postpone reproduction until the food supply recovers. Another reason women live longer than men may be that they invest more in raising children than men do.

Being married increases longevity among men by almost two years but *decreases* the lifespan of women by a year. Scientists believe the differences is caused by the stress of being married for women. However, if a wife is much younger than her husband, her longevity is not affected by marriage. Memory loss is an early sign of aging, and the incidence of cognitive decline and Alzheimer's disease are increasing as people live longer. Diabetes, high blood pressure, and strokes are the main causes of cognitive decline. In addition to Alzheimer's, three other cognitive disorders are associated with the accumulation of proteins in the brain. These include amyotrophic lateral sclerosis (ALS or Lou Gehrig's Disease), Huntington's disease, and Parkinson's disease. These disorders are caused by a different process than the cognitive decline associated with aging.

4

MENTAL AND PHYSICAL EXAMS

Studies show that individuals who visit a primary care physician annually live significantly longer than those who don't. Getting an annual exam increases the detection of emotional or medical conditions, improving the chances of successful treatment. Primary care physicians offer mental and physical examinations as part of their practice. Research has found that adding ten primary care physicians to a city with a population of one hundred thousand increased the average life expectancy of the residents by more than fifty-one days. In contrast, increasing the number of specialized physicians in the same city extended the longevity of these individuals by only nineteen days. Primary care physicians offer cancer screening and early diagnosis of mental and physical problems, giving patients a better chance of undergoing successful treatment before a health problem becomes life threatening. Unfortunately, the increase in general care doctors, pediatricians, or internal medicine physicians in the United States has not kept pace with population growth, so the number of primary care physicians per one hundred thousand persons in America has decreased from forty-seven to forty-one in recent decades. One reason for this decrease is that financial incentives lure physicians toward lucrative specialties such as cardiology or orthopedic surgery rather than general practice. Also, prestige is lower and burnout higher among primary care physicians compared with medical specialists.

However, seeing a primary care physician who knows your medical history and can provide diagnostic and medical care on a regular basis is critical to early detection and treatment of serious health issues, contributing to a long healthy life. Before a scheduled physical examination, a primary care physician will have the patient come to his or her office, so his assistant may collect blood and urine samples to assess vascular inflammation, clotting functions, lipid and glucose levels (fats and sugars in the blood), and check for signs of diabetes in the patient's urine. Older adults may need to visit their primary care physician more often because they are at risk of developing more serious health problems. Before beginning the physical exam, many physicians conduct a mental status evaluation to determine the cognitive and emotional condition of their patient.

Mental Status Exam. The majority of primary care physicians perform a mental status examination if their patient is older or they detect signs he or she is losing cognitive functions, experiencing significant mood changes, or having perceptual problems, to detect mental, emotional, or sensory issues. The mental status examination includes observations of the patient's appearance, behavior, motor movements, perceptions, mood, attention span, short-term memory, reasoning ability, comprehension, and judgment. The mental status exam is a subjective assessment of the patient's cognitive abilities and mood. During a mental status exam, the physician should consider the patient's culture, primary language, educational level, and current stresses when making an evaluation of functioning to rule out extraneous factors that may mimic mental or emotional problems. The physician should also inquire about substance abuse, current social relationships, neurological functions, and emotional status. The doctor will also note the patient's hygiene, social behavior, speech patterns, emotional status, and thought processes to determine if he or she is oriented in person, place, and time. If there are signs of mental or emotional problems, the physician will question the patient about feelings, perceptions, relationships, decision processes, and whether the patient is alert, oriented, able to recall recent events, and understands simple questions. The mental status examination is designed to detect whether a patient is suffering from cognitive decline, emotional problems, or a developing neurological condition, so the issue can be addressed by a psychiatrist. After the mental status examination, the physician will collect a medical history, including the patient's family history of disease.

Medical History. A complete medical history includes a list of familial diseases and chronic personal health problems such as high blood pressure, diabetes, heart disease, kidney or liver problems, and autoimmune disorders. The patient's complete medical history is important because if diseases occur in the family, he or she has an increased risk of developing the illness. For example, substance abuse is common in some families, so a physician should be careful when prescribing pain medication to these patients. The primary care doctor will also discuss prescription medications and supplements the patient is taking, including vitamins, minerals, herbs, and over-the-counter medicines. Then, the primary care physician will inquire whether the patient had any serious childhood illnesses such as mumps, measles, pneumonia, or tuberculosis, and explore how these diseases resolved and whether the patient might have recurring medical issues as a result. Most primary care physicians will review the patient's vaccination history and bring it up to date as needed. The doctor will also inquire about current health problems and prior surgical procedures, especially if the patient experienced complications such as bleeding, slow healing, residual pain, or stiffness. Once the mental status examination and medical history are complete, the physician will begin the physical examination.

Physical Examination. The purpose of a physical exam is to assess a patient's current health, detect early signs of developing medical problems, and treat any health issues before they become life-threatening. During a physical examination, the primary care physician evaluates a patient's general health, checks organ functions, notes symptoms, and any patient concerns. A comprehensive physical examination includes a review of prior medical conditions, the patient's current lifestyle, symptoms, and complaints. The examining physician will also assess vital signs, including blood pressure, heart rate, respiratory rate, temperature, height, and weight. There are several components to a complete physical examination, including observations of the patient's appearance, examination of his or her eyes, ears, nose, and throat, listening to the heart and lungs, examining the abdomen for tenderness, assessing muscle and joint function, and checking reflexes and coordination. The primary care physician will also examine the patient's skin for lesions or abnormalities that may indicate skin cancer and refer him or her to a dermatologist for treatment. After age forty, a physical examination may include screening for colon, breast, or prostate cancer, depending on family history and sex of the patient. Based on these observations and evaluations, the primary care physician may order vision, hearing, or electrocardiogram screening to determine whether a patient is at risk for sensory loss or heart disease.

Following the physical examination, the primary care physician will discuss the findings with the patient and make recommendations to address any problems, mitigate symptoms, or refer the patient to a specialist. The physical examination may also include a chest X-ray, a comprehensive blood analysis, and an electrocardiogram (EKG). For women, the primary care physician may order a mammogram, perform a breast examination, collect a Pap smear, perform a pelvic examination, and test for osteoporosis if the woman is over sixty-five or has a family history of osteoporosis. For men, the doctor may perform a prostate examination and order an ultrasound to measure aortic functioning, a colorectal cancer screen, a chest X-ray, a test for diabetes, hepatitis, and a screen for sexually transmitted diseases and HIV. Suppose a male patient is over seventy or has a family history of osteoporosis. In that case, the physician will usually order a bone density test to determine whether the patient is at risk of fractures. There is negligible risk from undergoing a physical examination, although minor discomfort occurs from drawing blood, and some women experience breast pain during the mammogram. If warranted, a chest X-ray will be ordered to screen for lung cancer or heart disease, especially if the patient smokes or lives with someone who uses tobacco.

Chest X-ray. An X-ray produces images of the patient's heart, lungs, vessels, and bones in the chest and spine. Emergency room physicians typically order a chest X-ray when a patient enters the hospital complaining of chest pain or shortness of breath to check for heart problems, pneumonia, or cancer. Serial X-rays may be obtained to determine whether a particular medical issue is worsening or resolving. X-ray images of the chest can reveal the condition of a patient's lungs, detect signs of cancer, an unresolved infection, or an air space around a lung, which can cause it to collapse. A chest X-ray can also detect changes in the shape or size of the heart. Additionally, an X-ray image may detect an aneurysm or other developing vascular problem. The X-ray may also show calcium deposits in the body, which indicate vessel damage or residue from a prior infection. Also, signs of prior fractures or developing osteoporosis may appear on an X-ray. Finally, a chest X-ray may be ordered after a pacemaker or catheter is placed to confirm proper positioning. In addition to a chest X-ray, the primary care physician will usually order a metabolic blood analysis to check for symptoms of Type 2 diabetes, blood vessel inflammation, and heart disease.

Metabolic Analysis. A comprehensive blood analysis helps physicians estimate the likelihood a patient will develop diabetes, cardiovascular disease, or have a stroke. Blood analysis can also detect signs of vascular inflammation and potential heart disease. The metabolic report analyzes several factors, including blood lipids, LDL and HDL levels and ratios, platelet size, glucose and vitamin levels, coagulation functions, general blood chemistry, thyroid status, iron metabolism, and levels of prostate specific antigens (PSA). Additionally, a metabolic analysis will assess the patient's blood pH, glucose levels, and specific gravity of the urine. Finally, a metabolic blood analysis will assess the likelihood of the patient developing heart disease by measuring inflammation of blood vessels and the risk of developing type 2 diabetes by measuring his or her sensitivity to insulin. In addition to a metabolic analysis of the patient's blood, a physician may order an electrocardiogram to assess the current functioning of the patient's heart.

Electrocardiogram (EKG). An EKG records electrical activity in a patient's heart to assess his or her potential for having a heart attack or to detect irregular heartbeats. This test is ordered to measure the rate and regularity of heart functioning. An EKG is recommended if a patient has had a prior heart attack, or is experiencing chest pain, dizziness, lightheadedness, fast pulse rate, shortness of breath, weakness, or fatigue. There is no risk associated with having an EKG and only minor discomfort during the procedure. The test can be performed in a physician's office, a clinic, or hospital. For older patients (females over sixty-five, males over seventy, or patients with a family history of osteoporosis), a bone density scan is recommended to determine whether a patient's bones are strong enough to resist fractures during a fall.

Bone Density Test. A bone density scan is a painless way to check bone strength. A bone density test measures the strength and mineral content of bones to determine if a patient is developing osteoporosis or other conditions that can weaken bones. The test uses X-rays to measure bone density among patients who are at risk for osteoporosis, such as post-menopausal females or older males to determine their bone strength and whether they are at risk of fractures from falling. If bone density is low, exercise, medication and calcium supplements may be recommended to strengthen bones. A bone density scan is recommended for females over sixty-five, males over seventy, individuals over fifty who have suffered broken bones in the past, patients where osteoporosis runs in their family, and older individuals who have lost more than an inch and one-half in height from their stature when they were twenty years old. Also, patients who smoke, drink large amounts of alcohol, have a vitamin D deficiency, or take immunosuppressants, seizure medications, or blood thinners should have their bone density measured annually. The test takes about one-half hour and is painless. Women who are pregnant should *not* undergo a bone density test because exposure to radiation may damage her fetus. Female patients should also have a mammogram annually after age forty to detect signs of breast cancer.

Mammogram. A mammogram involves an X-ray of the female patient's breasts to screen for cancer or other medical conditions. A mammogram may detect signs of breast cancer before serious symptoms appear. Detecting cancer at an early stage can save lives. Risks of a mammogram involve exposure to low levels of radiation, but the benefits outweigh any potential harm, because if breast cancer is detected early, it can often be treated by surgery before malignancy spreads and become life threatening. Mammograms should be scheduled at least a week before the onset of a menstrual period, and the patient should not use deodorant the day of the mammogram because it may interfere with collecting a clear image. A mammogram is uncomfortable for many women because the breasts must be compressed to produce a clear image. For male patients, a prostate examination and PSA test should be ordered after age fifty to screen for cancer.

Prostate Examination. There are two different tests used in checking for prostate cancer. One involves measuring prostate specific antigen (PSA) in the patient's blood, and the other test requires feeling the prostate with a physician's gloved finger searching for potential abnormalities. An unusual condition of the prostate during physical examination or elevated PSA may indicate the existence of prostate cancer and require a biopsy to confirm the condition. During a prostate exam the physician inserts a gloved finger into the rectum to feel the prostate and detect abnormalities. If a male patient has a family history of prostate cancer, he should begin prostate exams around age forty, while other males should begin scheduling prostate exams at age fifty. The prostate test should not be confused with a colonoscopy. The prostate examination checks for prostate cancer, while a colonoscopy screens for cancer of the gut. You should abstain from sex for two days prior to having a prostate exam, because ejaculation can elevate PSA levels and affect the results. If the patient's PSA level is high or the physician detects abnormalities in the prostate, a biopsy of the prostate or an MRI may be ordered to determine whether prostate cancer is developing and requires treatment by surgery, radiation, or drugs. Should everyone have a physical exam?

Who Needs a Physical Exam? The American Medical Association recommends that infants, children, adolescents, and adults should have an annual physical examination to detect changes in their health and uncover signs of developing disease. Older people may need to visit their primary care physician more often. Anyone experiencing symptoms such as localized pain, joint or muscle stiffness, fever, shortness of breath, skin lesions that don't heal, or other symptoms should visit a primary care physician immediately. Frequent health examinations are critical when an individual has a personal or family history of diabetes, high blood pressure, or cancer, to detect developing issues before they become serious.

Individuals may be referred to a physician for a pre-employment physical examination before beginning a new job, or when a student wants to participate in a school sport. When meeting with a primary care physician, patients should bring a list of medications they are taking, note any allergies they have, and gather records of blood pressure or blood sugar levels collected over the prior year, a list of questions they want to ask the physician, and the names, addresses, phone numbers, and reasons why they have seen any other physician in the past year. A physician's assistant may measure the patient's height and weight, check blood pressure and heart rate, assess the patient's lifestyle, discuss medical care preferences, the status of a living will, and review any current health concerns before the patient sees the physician. The physician's assistant may also inquire about any pain the patient is experiencing, the duration and intensity of the pain, the location of the pain, and whether it is associated with any particular activity such as exercise or eating. Finally, the assistant will want to know what the patient does to relieve his or her pain. For example, does rest, medication, exercise, or a particular body position minimize or alleviate the pain?

Summary. Infants, children, adolescents, and adults should schedule regular physical and mental examinations to screen for developing health problems so they can be treated before serious complications develop. Older individuals should visit their primary care physician more often as needed. Anyone experiencing pain, fever, shortness of breath, skin lesions that don't heal, or other symptoms should visit a primary care physician to have the problem assessed. A comprehensive examination includes a mental status interview, medical history, chest X-ray, cardiometabolic blood analysis, EKG, and testing of reflexes and motor functions. For women, a mammogram, Pap smear, pelvic examination, and test for osteoporosis is recommended. For men, a prostate examination, PSA test, and ultrasound to measure aortic functioning is usually ordered. Regular mental and physical examinations detect health problems early and offer patients a better chance to receive successful treatment before an illness becomes life-threatening.

5

DIET AND LONGEVITY

To live a long healthy life, individuals should consume a diet that includes fresh fruit and vegetables, low-fat cheese, fish, vegetable fats such as avocado or olive oil, seeds, nuts, and multigrain crackers or bread. The Mediterranean diet, which originated among ancient Greek, Moroccan, Roman, and Spanish cultures is a healthy diet that includes low fat cheese, fish such as tuna, bass, anchovies, salmon, or sardines, fresh fruit, vegetables, legumes such as lentils and beans, occasional lean red meat, whole gains, nuts, olive oil, and dry roasted chicken. Consuming a Mediterranean diet reduces the risk of developing cancer, high blood pressure, heart disease, and stroke, while promoting weight loss and general health. Scientists have shown that rats raised on a Mediterranean diet, which included olive oil rather than butter, vegetables at every meal, plant-based proteins such as lentils, fish, fresh fruit rather than sweet fatty desserts, and nuts or seeds instead of salted potato chips, improved the animal's memory, lowered their risk of mental decline, and increased longevity. Eating a Mediterranean diet also lowers the risk of developing

Type 2 diabetes. Researchers have found that eating fresh fruit rich in antioxidants lowers blood sugar levels, reduces the risk of Type 2 diabetes, and promotes overall health.

Studies have found that consuming fresh vegetables such as broccoli, cauliflower, kale, and Brussels sprouts can reduce the risk of certain cancers. Adding fresh fish, such as salmon or sardines, which are rich in omega-3 fatty acids, to a diet keeps the heart healthy, while consuming mushrooms reduces the effects of stress on health. Cooking with spices such as cinnamon also reduces blood sugar fluctuations, adding turmeric and vitamin D to a diet can help control inflammation in blood vessels, and drinking green tea can limit cell damage from aging and increase longevity. Physicians recommend that individuals avoid becoming overweight because excess fat damages heart health. Nutritionists recommend that people stop eating when they are 80 percent satiated so they don't overeat, gain weight, and increase the risk of heart disease or stroke. Avoiding fatty meats, processed foods such as salty potato chips or sweets such as cake or cookies, and generally limiting the amount of sugar and salt in a diet will help individuals live a long healthy life. The secret to eating a healthy diet is to include a variety of fresh fruit and vegetables, fish, whole grains, and legumes, and to avoid processed foods such as bacon, hot dogs, salty potato chips, cake, or cookies, which contain added salt, sugar, and harmful dyes or preservatives. A healthy diet should include different foods.

Eat A Variety of Foods. The Mediterranean diet includes fish, lean red meat, whole-grain pasta or bread, vegetables, fresh fruits, nuts, seeds, and avocado or olive oil. A healthy diet should include fish rich in omega-3 fatty acids, such as salmon and mackerel, and legumes, such as chickpeas, lentils, and beans, which provide vegetable protein for building and maintaining muscles. Nutritionists suggest people avoid eating processed meats such as bacon, ham, hot dogs, or bologna because they contain unhealthy additives. A healthy diet may include lean red meats such as roasted lamb, broiled filet, or braised veal cutlets. Still, meats that contain marbled fat should be avoided because they can cause weight gain, which is associated with developing high blood pressure, stroke, heart disease, and some types of cancer. Other sources of healthy protein include low-fat cheese and yogurt, which provide muscle-building amino acids, calcium for strong bones, and probiotics to support gut health. Nuts such as almonds, walnuts, cashews, or pecans add fiber, flavor, and healthy fats to the Mediterranean diet. Fresh oranges, figs, apricots, and grapes offer a healthy alternative to sugary desserts such as cake, cookies, pies, or pudding. The Mediterranean diet involves more than just eating the right foods; it is a way of life that includes spending time with family and friends in a relaxed atmosphere of love and laughter.

Dining with Family and Friends. The Mediterranean diet combines a relaxed atmosphere, healthy food, and companionship to enhance dining and support mental and physical health. Sharing food, wine, conversation, and fellowship over a meal served on dishes inspired by the Mediterranean Sea creates a relaxed social experience conducive to good health. Fresh flowers, elegant glassware, and candles can enhance the atmosphere and complement healthy food. Mediterranean living is characterized by healthy dining, friendly socializing, and informal manners. A typical meal includes local white or red wines that complement the flavors of fresh wholesome food. Mediterranean dining is relaxed, encouraging meaningful conversation and warm companionship. The meal often ends with a light dessert of nuts, cheese, and fruit rather than a sweet, fatty dessert. Another secret of a Mediterranean diet is moderation. A meal containing fresh fruit, vegetables, fish, nuts, olive oil, low-fat cheese, and a glass of wine keeps people healthy, avoids weight gain, and extends longevity. In contrast, overeating, being overweight, and drinking large amounts of alcohol will shorten life and increase the likelihood of developing a stroke, heart disease, inflamed blood vessels, and some forms of cancer.

The toxicity of alcohol varies widely among ethnic groups. For example, Orientals and Native Americans are affected by small amounts of alcohol, while white Americans tolerate consuming modest amounts of alcohol. The World Health Organization recommends that adult white men limit their alcohol intake to two drinks daily, that white women should limit their alcohol intake to one drink daily, and individuals over fifty would be wise to limit their intake of alcohol to one drink a day. A standard drink is defined as twelve ounces of beer, five ounces of wine, or one and one-half ounces of liquor. A good way to measure whether a person is consuming too many calories is to calculate their Body Mass Index (BMI) and compare it with charts that define normal, overweight, and obese body weight. Physicians recommend staying within the normal BMI range to enjoy good health and increased longevity.

Body Mass Index (BMI). Excess bodyweight decreases health and longevity. Obesity is assessed using BMI, which is calculated by dividing body weight in pounds by the square of a person's height in inches and multiplying that number by 703. To calculate an individual's BMI, divide his or her weight in pounds by the square of the person's height in inches and divide that number by 703. There are apps available online that calculate BMI, but to understand the process, assume you are seventy-two inches tall (six feet) and weigh one hundred fifty pounds, two hundred pounds, or two hundred fifty pounds, then your BMI would be calculated as follows:

150/72 x 72 x 703 = 150/5184 x 703=150/7.37= 20.3

200/72 x 72 x 703 = 200/5184x703=200/7.37=27.1

250/72 x 72 x 703 = 250/5184 x 703=250/7.37=33.9

BMI Normal and Abnormal Ranges

18.5-24.5	Normal
25-29.9	Overweight
30-38.9	Obese

These calculations and charts are valid for both males and females. If your BMI is within the normal range, you are eating and exercising properly to achieve a balance between food intake and activity, and a healthy BMI. However, if your BMI is in the overweight or obese range, you are eating too many of the wrong foods, consuming to many sweets or fats, and exercising too little. Eating excess calories and exercising infrequently can cause weight gain, which is associated with the development of heart disease, cancer, and shorter life expectancy. Fatty meats contain more calories than vegetable proteins, such as lentils or beans, and healthy carbohydrates, such as whole grains or seeds. Limiting the amount of alcohol you drink, avoiding cream, fatty meats, processed foods, and butter, eating fresh fruit, vegetables, whole grain bread, and exercising every day will increase your chances of staying within the normal range of BMI and living a long, healthy life.

Individuals who eat a Mediterranean diet are less likely to develop cardiovascular disease, cancer, Alzheimer's, or Type 2 diabetes compared with people who consume high fat diets which contain processed foods with excess sugar, salt, and fat.

Consuming a Mediterranean diet also reduces the risk of dementia, childhood asthma, metabolic syndrome, and arthritis, especially among people who exercise daily. The keys to enjoying a healthy life are eating a variety of fresh foods, cooking with fresh herbs, exercising regularly, and sharing a meal with friends in a relaxed atmosphere.

Dieticians recommend that individuals consume healthy fats such as olive or avocado oil rather than butter to reduce LDL cholesterol levels. Unsaturated vegetable fats are liquid at room temperature and are suitable for you. However, nutritionists recommend avoiding coconut oil or hydrogenated fats that are solid at room temperature, because they are associated with heart disease, stroke, and some types of cancer. Eat low-fat cheese or yogurt to increase your calcium and protein intake and support muscle growth and bone development. Avoid flavored yogurts with added sugar because these foods are not healthy for individuals prone to developing type 2 diabetes. A good general dietary rule is to make your meal half fruits and vegetables, one-quarter whole grains, and one-quarter lean protein. Cook with tomato sauce or olive oil rather than butter, animal fat, or hydrogenated oils for better health and a longer life. Substitute lentils and beans for fatty red meat and avoid processed foods high in saturated fats, sugar, and salt. For dessert, eat fresh fruit and cheese rather than cookies, cake, ice cream, or pudding. Limit fried foods and salty potato chips because they are loaded with salt and saturated fats which can shorten lifespan and damage health. Typical Mediterranean meals for breakfast, lunch, and dinner include the following dishes.

Breakfast. The first meal of the day in many Mediterranean countries features fresh fruit, whole grains, nuts, olive oil, or low-fat unsweetened dairy products such as Greek yogurt with nuts, or seeds, and hummus. Other breakfast alternatives include cottage cheese and berries, or a hard-boiled egg with low-fat cheese and fresh fruit.

Berries, honey, eggs poached in tomato sauce, spinach and cheese muffins, a vegetable omelet cooked in olive oil, avocado toast, or a bowl of quinoa with fruit, nuts, and milk can make a healthy breakfast. Other healthy breakfast choices include vegetables and egg frittata, Greek yogurt with walnuts, berries, and seeds, or sweet potato hash and a poached egg. Rolled oats with fresh fruit, low-fat milk, almonds, and honey can make a healthy first meal of the day. Breakfast foods to avoid include refined white bread toast, bacon, ham, butter, and whole milk. A Mediterranean lunch generally includes vegetables, a salad, low-fat cheese, and fresh fruit.

Lunch. Mediterranean lunches often feature a grilled vegetable wrap, grilled chicken, hummus, and vegetables on whole-grain bread, a low-fat cheese salad, tuna and bean salad, or baked stuffed peppers. Other healthy lunches include a green salad with roast chicken or salmon, chickpea and farro salad, lentil and tuna salad, or white bean soup and salad. Similar ingredients are included in Mediterranean dinners.

Dinner. For the evening meal, Mediterranean diners often enjoy baked salmon and vegetables, shrimp and pasta, grilled lamb chops, stuffed baked zucchini, roasted chicken with yogurt, eggplant parmesan, couscous salad, garlic roasted broccoli, rice pilaf, or baked zucchini with yogurt. Other good choices for a delicious healthy evening meal include lentil soup with spinach, baked cod with roasted potatoes and asparagus, shrimp and farro, roasted chicken with root vegetables, or Brussels sprouts with baked salmon and quinoa salad. The Mediterranean diet includes fresh fruit, vegetables, fish, nuts, and low-fat cheese or yogurt. A healthy diet rejects fatty, salty, and sweet foods. The Mediterranean diet offers healthy desserts that complement the meal.

Desserts. Mediterranean desserts are light and refreshing rather than sweet and fatty. Delicious light desserts include nut pastry, fresh fruit salad with honey, orange almond cake, or fig walnut biscotti. Mediterranean snacks include seasonal nuts, vegetables, olive oil, and fruits.

Snacks. Hummus, fresh fruit, nuts, unsweetened Greek yogurt, green stuffed olives, fresh tomatoes, beans, carrots, herb-roasted chickpeas, berries, a hard-boiled egg, and multigrain unsalted crackers make a delicious and colorful snack plate. Red pepper and walnut dip can add spice to any snack. Marinated olives and lemon slices make a zesty treat, paired with whole-grain unsalted crackers. Finally, baked zucchini with yogurt dip makes a flavorful snack. To live longer, there are several foods you should avoid, especially after age fifty.

Foods to Avoid. Individuals who want to eat a healthy diet should limit their consumption of fried foods, which dramatically increase calories without adding nutritional value. Also, avoid eating refined white pasta and foods with added sugar or salt. When you are out for an evening at a restaurant, order a salad instead of French fries or onion rings. Avoid sweet tea, sugary soft drinks, and sweet lemonade. A good rule is to limit your intake of sugar to no more than 10 percent of your daily calories.

Have a glass of water or wine with dinner rather than sweet drinks. Avoid processed foods such as tomato sauces, granola bars, and sweetened breakfast cereals because they contain extra calories without added nutrients. Check the labels on processed foods and avoid any product that contains large amounts of sugar, salt, or fat. Read nutrition levels carefully to avoid consuming foods with several different types of sugar, because that's how producers load foods with calories without alerting the consumer that the main ingredient is sugar. If you aren't familiar with an ingredient listed on the package or can't pronounce it, avoid buying the food because it's not likely to be healthy. Other foods to avoid are frozen pizza, canned soups, salted nuts, salted crackers, and potato chips.

Substitute a banana on toast for jam at breakfast. Avoid using coconut oil; choose avocado or olive oil instead. Don't eat processed grains such as white rice or pasta; instead, cook whole-wheat pasta or brown rice to complement low-fat protein, such as broiled fish or roasted lean meat. Switch to whole-grain bread; it has twice the fiber and extra protein compared with white bread. Avoid processed meats such as bacon, hot dogs, or sausage because they contains fats, additives, and preservatives that are unhealthy and associated with some types of cancer. A healthy diet should limit trans fats, which are created when hydrogen is added to liquid vegetable oils to make them solid at room temperature. To prepare a Mediterranean diet, buy good kitchen tools to produce healthy, tasty meals. Use a sharp, high-quality chef's knife for chopping and slicing fruits, vegetables, and meats. A durable wood cutting board is helpful for keeping a knife sharp. A grater is essential for preparing cheese and garlic additives to foods. A sturdy non-stick skillet and pans will help you prepare pasta, soups, chops, and fish.

Summary. Studies show that a diet rich in vegetable proteins such as lentils or beans, unsaturated fats such as avocado or olive oil, fish, lean red meat, low fat cheese, and fresh fruits and vegetables is healthier than one which contains processed foods high in salt, sugar, preservatives, and saturated fats. A Mediterranean diet will reduce the risk of age-related diseases and increase longevity. Consuming unsaturated fats such as olive or avocado oil is associated with good health and a longer life. Eating plant protein such as lentils or beans supports health and longevity. Choose foods that contain vitamin D and calcium, such as milk, yogurt, cheese, salmon, tuna, and eggs, to promote strong bones and mobility while moderating vascular inflammation. Individuals who want to live a long, healthy life should avoid foods containing saturated fats because they are associated with heart disease and shorter life spans.

Finally, eating processed meats such as bacon, ham, sausage, salami, or hot dogs and drinking sugary beverages are associated with premature death. Consuming foods high in sugar can increase the risk of developing Type 2 diabetes. Eating foods containing emulsifiers, such as carrageenan and modified starch, which are often added to commercial meat stocks, dairy desserts, and sauces, increases the risk of Type 2 diabetes. Additionally, sweeteners, food colorings, and acidifiers found in commercial sodas increase the risk of Type 2 diabetes. Studies show that not only are many individual foods toxic to health, but combinations of additives may interact to cause premature death and increase the risk of developing many diseases. Research suggests these additives may disrupt the gut's microbiome and reduce insulin sensitivity among individuals who consume them regularly, which can lead to the development of Type 2 diabetes or other diseases. Eating a Mediterranean diet will promote health and longevity.

6

EXERCISE AND AGING

Living longer involves more than adding a few years to a person's life; it's also about being healthy enough to enjoy the extra time. Exercise maintains strength, cardiovascular health, mobility, fitness, and longevity. The keys to fitness training are proper technique and consistency. Effective exercise requires alternating strength training with walking, jogging, cycling, or swimming to maintain balance, cardiovascular fitness, and mobility. No one exercise will build and maintain strength and cardiovascular health. A variety of foods are necessary to stay strong, fit, and heart-healthy. After exercising for a while, people discover that repeating an activity becomes easier, so they add weight, increase repetitions, or walk, swim, cycle, or jog further and faster to enhance fitness. As people exercise, they should pay attention to any pain and avoid activities that cause discomfort or injury. If an individual experiences joint or muscle stiffness or pain, he or she should modify or avoid that routine for a few days until the stiffness or pain disappears. Focusing on the proper form for each exercise is also essential because doing an exercise correctly helps prevent stiffness, pain, and injury. Alternate weight training and cardiovascular exercise, so the body has time to recover from each activity. Aerobic exercise helps maintain a healthy heart, prevent high blood pressure, and support fitness, while strength training builds muscle mass to make the body stronger.

Strength Training. Building muscle mass is essential to developing a strong body, maintaining flexibility, balance, and avoiding falls. Weight training stimulates the growth of muscles, improves balance, increases bone density, lowers the risk of injury from falling, improves health, and produces a feeling of well-being. Maintaining muscle mass also helps regulate blood sugar levels and may prevent the development of Type 2 diabetes. Strength training can help prevent the accumulation of dangerous fat. Being stronger enhances independence and allows older individuals to remain in their homes longer without assistance. Weight training also helps older adults maintain stability and balance to prevent falls and injuries, and promotes joint flexibility. In contrast, losing muscle mass with age limits mobility, impairs balance, reduces flexibility, and increases the risk of fractures from falls. Strength training stimulates healthy muscle growth by enlarging muscle fibers and increasing strength. Being strong and flexible helps with everyday tasks such as lifting grocery sacks, climbing stairs, getting out of an auto, and getting up from a chair. Building and maintaining muscle strength allows older adults to live independently for years longer, and strong muscles help maintain stability and flexibility for walking, climbing stairs, and moving around the house or yard. Weight training builds and maintains bone density, helping prevent osteoporosis and reducing the risk of fractures among older individuals. Finally, strength training enhances flexibility.

Flexibility. Strength training helps maintain flexibility, reduces the likelihood of falls, prevents injury, and preserves independence for older adults. Stretching and rotating joints enhance and maintain flexibility and improve balance. Incorporating strength training, cardiovascular exercise, and mobility exercises into a daily routine will enhance long-term health, fitness, and longevity. Exercise also releases endorphins which reduce stress, enhance mood, and support cognitive functioning. Climbing stairs or walking requires leg strength, balance, and stability. However, as adults age, their balance deteriorates, increasing the risk of falls, fractures, and death. Slower reflexes limit the body's ability to balance, increasing the risk of falls. Aging also reduces a person's sense of where his or her body is in space, making it more challenging to adjust to sudden environmental changes, such as walking on uneven ground or encountering a slippery surface, which can cause a dangerous fall. Standing on one leg (like a stork) is an effective way to improve and maintain balance and flexibility. Building strong muscles also contributes to metabolic health.

Metabolic Health. Muscles require energy to function, and strong muscles stimulate body metabolism, help maintain healthy body weight, reduce the risk of Type 2 diabetes, and lower the likelihood of developing heart disease among older adults. Increased muscle mass helps regulate basal metabolic rate (BMR), which is the energy required to support basic physiological functions such as breathing, blood circulation, and cell activity. Individuals with more muscle mass have a higher BMR, which means they burn more calories and can more easily avoid weight gain associated with high blood pressure, stroke, and heart disease. Muscles are also a primary storage area for blood sugar and larger muscles help regulate blood sugar levels and avoid the development of Type 2 diabetes. The human body metabolizes carbohydrates into glucose, which is then transported to muscles by insulin produced in the pancreas, where it is stored and used during daily activities. Stronger muscles also help regulate the production of hormones such as testosterone and growth factors, reducing the effect of aging by increasing energy and maintaining a sense of well-being. When undergoing strength training, it's important to measure progress by recording the weight lifted and the number of repetitions for each exercise.

Measuring Strength. Increased fitness can be assessed by recording the weight and repetitions a person does before becoming fatigued. When a person first begins exercising, he or she should note the weight lifted and the number of repetitions to establish a baseline. After exercising for a few weeks, increasing the number of repetitions and the amount of weight used will stimulate muscle growth and enhance strength. Increasing the weight used and number of repetitions is called progressive overload; it occurs when a person increases the difficulty level of an exercise. Increasing the amount of weight lifted and the number of repetitions performed improves fitness, and recording progress will increase motivation, because these activities signal increased fitness. Endurance is a measure of the body's ability to lift more weight and do more repetitions before becoming fatigued. In addition to becoming stronger, another benefit of weight training is improved balance and flexibility.

Measuring Balance and Flexibility. Strength, stability, and flexibility are key components of longevity and good health. To assess balance, an individual should record the time he or she can stand on one foot. Begin with fifteen seconds and gradually increase the duration of standing on one foot up to thirty seconds or more. To monitor flexibility, note range of motion, which is how many degrees a person can move their arm or leg during each exercise, and the ease of movement when performing each activity. A person should pay attention every day to how they feel while exercising and during daily living. Weight training and aerobic exercises will become easier over time, and climbing stairs, moving packages, or bending down to pick something up will also feel more natural after a few months of exercise. Another measure of fitness and flexibility is how quickly a person recovers following strenuous exercise. Feeling less stiff or sore after rigorous exercise means a person is becoming fitter. Weight training builds and maintains muscle mass, improves metabolic function, enhances balance, helps avoid falls, and will extend the time a person can function independently and enjoy living. Developing balance and coordination requires performing specific exercises.

Enhancing Balance and Coordination. To increase ankle flexibility, face a wall, place one hand on the wall, stand flat on your feet, and lift your body as high as possible onto your toes twenty times. This exercise will strengthen calf muscles, enhance ankle flexibility, and increase balance and coordination. Next, stand in the middle of a room on one leg for thirty seconds while holding the other leg in front of your body and extend your arms straight out. In the beginning, try to stand on one leg (like a stork) for fifteen seconds, using your extended arms and the leg in front for balance. After you balance for fifteen or more seconds on one leg, stand on the other leg, holding the free leg in front of your body, extend your arms to the side, and balance for fifteen or more seconds. Repeat standing on each leg like a stork two times for fifteen or more seconds to enhance balance. Next, walk down a hall and back twice for a minimum of twenty-five steps, placing the heel of one foot directly in front of the other foot while walking. This exercise will increase balance and help avoid falling while walking or hiking. In addition to strength training, balance exercises, and coordination training, cardiovascular fitness is essential to maintain health and longevity.

Aerobic Exercise. Walking, jogging, swimming, or cycling at least three times a week for between thirty and forty-five minutes will improve heart health, promote flexible blood vessels, and regulate blood pressure. Consistent cardiovascular exercise increases fitness, maintains joint flexibility, supports general health, and enhances independence. Aerobic exercise also maintains joint flexibility. There are several rules you should keep in mind when planning a longevity exercise routine. Rule one is to alternate weight training and aerobic exercise to achieve muscle strength and endurance. Rule two is to plan an exercise program you can maintain for a lifetime. It won't do any good to exercise strenuously for a month and then quit because the program is too complicated. Rule three is not to exercise to the point where you become stiff or suffer pain, because that will make you stop exercising and you will lose the fitness gains you worked so hard to attain. Alternating cardiovascular exercise with strength training builds and maintains fitness, increases endurance, and improves balance and flexibility. Building good habits will help you maintain your exercise routine.

Habit Formation. Maintaining an exercise routine requires consistency, discipline, and motivation. It's essential to avoid injury, because nothing is more discouraging than hurting yourself and stopping exercising to recover. After all, you lose the fitness you worked so hard to achieve. In the beginning, plan to exercise for thirty minutes three or four times a week to build and maintain endurance. After a few weeks, increase the speed and duration of walking, cycling, or swimming until you achieve the desired level of fitness. During strength training, begin with a comfortable weight and gradually increase both the weight and the number of repetitions as your fitness improves. Schedule your exercise routine so it won't be interrupted by work or social obligations. Keep track of your progress to determine whether you are improving in strength and endurance. Exercise at the same time every day so fitness training becomes a habit. Schedule exercising early in the morning or late in the afternoon when there are few competing activities, so you have time to exercise every day. Plan your work and social schedules for other times to avoid skipping your exercise routine. Training with a friend will make you accountable and help motivate you to exercise every day. Reward yourself when you reach a milestone, such as a new weight level, more repetitions of a routine, or a longer and faster aerobic exercise by buying a new piece of exercise equipment or going out to lunch with a friend. Your exercise routine should include exercises that increase the strength, fitness, endurance, and flexibility of your core, legs, and arms.

Core Strength. The six basic exercises that increase core strength are sit-ups, bench presses, leg lifts, back exercises, neck lifts, and side stretches. To do a sit up, lay on a mat on your back, place your toes under a stationary bar, pull your upper body into a sitting position, and lower your body back onto the mat. Breath in, hold your breath, and breath out during successive sit-ups. Your writer is ninety-one and does two sets of thirty sit-ups (a total of sixty sit-ups) every other day. In addition to sit-ups, I perform twenty bench presses, lifting fifty pounds of weight three days a week. To exercise my back, I lay on my stomach on a mat and lift one leg and the opposite arm twenty times, and then do the same with the other leg and arm. To exercise my neck, I place a five-pound weight on one side of my head, lift the weight and my head twenty times, and repeat this exercise on the other side of my head. To strengthen my side muscles, I grip ten-pound weights in each hand alongside my body, lean to the right as far as possible, and then lean to the left as far as possible twenty times. In addition to muscle strength, it's also important to maintain leg flexibility.

Leg and Arm Strength and Mobility. Lie on your back on a pad, hold a ten-pound weight in each hand, extend your arms straight out as far as possible, and move the weights up and together over your body twenty times until they touch in the middle to strengthen your front shoulder muscles. To maintain knee flexibility, sit in a chair, attach a ten-pound weight to each ankle, and lift alternate legs with the weight attached twenty times. To enhance the flexibility in your ankles, place a hand on a wall in front of you and lift your body as high as possible on your toes twenty times. For arm strength and mobility, hold a ten-pound weight in each hand, sit in a chair, bend forward, and lift the weights as high as you can straight out to increase the strength and flexibility of your shoulder and back muscles. Next, while sitting in a chair, hold a ten-pound weight in one hand, lift that arm to shoulder height, bend the arm so your hand is straight up, and extend the arm and weight forward twenty times. This exercise will increase the strength and flexibility of your arm by moving it against resistance. To increase leg strength and mobility, sit in a chair and stand up 20 times without using your arms to lift yourself out of the chair. This exercise will make it easier to get out of a chair with less effort.

To increase the strength, flexibility, and mobility in your shoulders, hold a ten-pound weight in each hand while standing, lower your arms to your sides, and lift the weights straight out and up 20 times above your head. This exercise will increase the strength and flexibility of your shoulder muscles. Next, take a ten-pound weight in each hand, stand up, hold the weights in front of your body and lift them up and curl your arms into your body twenty times. Lifting weights this way will strengthen your biceps. To experience the benefit of strength training and cardiovascular exercise, you need to maintain a comfortable exercise routine for the rest of your life. Exercising is not effective if you only do it intermittently. You need to exercise every day, alternating strength training and aerobic exercises to achieve and maintain maximum fitness as you age. You cannot maintain fitness by exercising once in a while. You need to develop the habit of exercising daily to enjoy maximum benefits.

To maintain an exercise routine, it must be appropriate for your fitness level and age, or it won't be sustainable. Slow and steady exercising works better than attempting to become fit overnight. Becoming fit is a lifetime job.

Maintaining Fitness. Don't try to achieve quick results by exercising too hard. Slow and steady increases in weight lifted, number of repetitions, and length of aerobic training work best. Choose a time to exercise that will not be interrupted, such as first thing in the morning or in the late afternoon when you return home. Set consistent, achievable goals, and exercise with friends to increase your motivation and maintain consistency. Surround yourself with people who value fitness and exercise every day. Keep a log of your performance so you can record improvements. Remember that as individuals age, it's necessary to decrease the weight lifted or slow the pace of aerobic exercise while increasing repetitions or walking for a longer interval to achieve the same level of fitness. Choose low-impact aerobic exercises such as walking, swimming, cycling, or using an elliptical machine to enhance cardiovascular fitness without damaging knee joints. Avoid running marathons; they are for young and reckless individuals. Make certain to get at least eight or more hours of sleep every night. Building sustainable exercise and sleep habits will pay off with enhanced fitness, better health, and a longer life.

Summary. The most important causes of death among citizens of rich industrialized countries are cardiovascular disease and cancer. Nearly 70 percent of women and 65 percent of men die from these two diseases. Regular exercise reduces the risk of hypertension, Type 2 diabetes, heart disease, stroke, and certain types of cancer. Studies consistently show that regular exercise reduces the risk of death by more than 30 percent. Research shows that physical activity can extend life expectancy by four to seven years. Studies also show that people who perform aerobic exercises in addition to strength training live longer than individuals who do only weightlifting. Avoiding certain toxic behaviors will also increase longevity. For example, not smoking or being overweight, combined with exercise increases the life expectancy of men by an average of twelve years compared with men who smoke, are obese, and inactive. Men who didn't smoke, consumed a healthy diet, exercise, and drink only a moderate amount of alcohol increased their average life expectancy by more than eleven years compared with those who smoke, are overweight, consume a diet containing saturated fats and processed foods, and didn't exercise. For women, not smoking or being overweight, combined with exercise increased their life expectancy by an average of ten years compared with those who smoke, are obese, and inactive. Women who don't smoke, eat a healthy diet, exercise, and drink moderate amounts of alcohol increased their average life expectancy by more than nine years compared with women who smoked, were overweight, consumed a diet high in saturated fats and processed foods, and avoided physical exercise.

7

SOCIAL CONNECTIONS AND LONGEVITY

Research shows that good genetics, a safe environment, medical care, a healthy diet, and daily exercise contribute to living a long, healthy life. However, humans are social animals, so developing relationships decrease the risk of suffering a heart attack, having Type 2 diabetes, being depressed, or developing Alzheimer's disease. If you want to live a long healthy life, maintain social connections and live in a friendly community that supports an active lifestyle. Individuals with few social connections risk depression, mental decline, developing Alzheimer's disease, and dying young compared with individuals who have satisfying social connections. Unfortunately, opportunities for developing social relationships have declined in recent years, so modern adults spend more time alone, and report having fewer friends than individuals from earlier generations. Having few social connections increases the risk of developing a stroke by over 30 percent, raises the likelihood of dementia by fifty percent, and elevates the chance of dying early by twenty percent.

The number and kind of social connections a person develops depend on his or her ability to interact effectively with others and the social opportunities available. Good mental health requires making and maintaining connections with friends, family, co-workers, neighbors, and a romantic partner. If a person's social relationships are healthy, he or she feels loved, understood, and valued, has a sense of belonging, and is likely to live longer than someone with few social connections.

Friendships, family connections, romantic relationships, and social interactions give individuals extended longevity. Studies show that men with few social relationships are twice as likely to die young compared with men who have many social connections. For women, being socially isolated is even more dangerous; they are three times more likely to die over the following decade compared with women who have satisfying social connections. Not developing social relationships has nearly the same harmful effect as smoking, drinking excessive alcohol, or being obese. Strong connections with family and friends enhance the human immune system and support mental and physical health. Moreover, having social relationships helps people avoid illnesses and speeds recovery from sickness. Individuals with many social connections experience lower levels of stress and vascular inflammation than those with few social connections. However, not many people are aware that feeling lonely can be life-threatening or that social connections support physical and mental health.

Healthy Social Connections. The number and quality of social relationships needed for mental and physical health vary among individuals. Some people need several close social connections to avoid feeling lonely, while others find that a few friends are adequate to meet their social needs. Belonging to a group enhances physical and mental health. Many organizations can fulfill the need for social relationships, from book clubs to sports teams, but being part of a group helps people feel connected and extends their longevity. Healthy social relationships are reciprocal, but casual, one-sided connections are unlikely to satisfy a person's need for connection. The total number of social relationships is not so important as the quality of a person's connections to a few individuals. Social relationships ebb and flow during a lifetime, and an individual's need for social connections can change over time. To evaluate your own social connections, identify the top five relationships in your life and estimate their strength. Assess the meaningfulness of these relationships by estimating how important each connection is to you, and whether the social connection is reciprocal, essential, and fulfilling. There is an optimum number of social connections for every person. and different ways to achieve social, mental, and physical health because everyone has unique needs for companionship. Some people crave many relationships, while others need only a few strong connections to thrive. Some individuals seek many different relationships, while a fourth type of person may need only a few similar connections to feel fulfilled.

If you thrive on developing many casual relationships, you are probably a great party guest because you want to meet everyone, enjoy making the rounds, and love meeting new people. Individuals who need only a few connections to feel socially, mentally, and physically healthy may be shy, stay out of the spotlight, and make connections primarily with friends and family. A third group seeks variety and needs connections with different types of people to thrive, while a final group wants a few strong social contacts to feel socially healthy. How do scientists measure social connections?

Assessing Social Health. Measures of social health include the number and quality of relationships a person has with family, friends, a romantic partner, co-workers, and neighbors. However, having only a few social connections may cause loneliness, isolation, and stress, which increase the likelihood of premature death. An effective way to evaluate your social relationships is to imagine who you would call if you were going to the emergency room at a local hospital and needed emotional support. That person is someone you trust, and you should spend more time with him or her in the future to live a long healthy life. Another way to measure the adequacy of your social connections is to consider who you would invite to your birthday party. These individuals are not necessarily close friends, but are an important part of your social network, and associating with them supports your social, mental, and physical health. However, not all social connections are positive. Some individuals are abrasive, toxic, or destructive, and should be avoided because they will reduce your life expectancy. Social connections based on trust, love, and mutual respect enhance physical health, feelings of well-being, and longevity for most individuals, but complex relationships are destructive and will shorten life.

If you are not certain which type of social relationships are right for you, try the following experiment: connect with three new people in the next month, maintain at least three existing social relationships during that time, and spend an hour every day interacting with a friend or family member. If you find that meeting new people makes you feel better, then you probably need to increase the number of your social connections to live a long, healthy life. On the other hand, if you discover that meeting three new people in a month, maintaining three existing social connections, and interacting with a friend or family member every day is a burden, you probably don't need more social connections to feel good about yourself and maintain physical, mental, and social health. You should also consider whether you want to make all your connections with the same types of people or create more diversity in your relationships.

Some individuals make connections with people like themselves to feel comfortable, while others need a diverse group of social connections to thrive.

Being in a close relationship with another person is essential for social, mental, and physical health, but a romantic relationship is generally not enough to ensure social health. Humans need different types of connections, which is why people have friends who are younger, older, of different ethnic groups, and possess unique belief systems, because social diversity help people maintain good social, mental, and physical health. Developing good social health begins with understanding and accepting yourself. Feeling good about yourself and taking care of your own well-being are essential components of living a long, healthy life.

Developing Connections. Social connections are essential to mental and physical health. Maintain family relationships, develop close social connections with friends, and become part of a community to live a long, healthy life. Get involved in a church, a cooking class, a book club, a bridge group, or a children's organization to stay connected with your community and live longer. Develop social relationships with many individuals and experiment with different groups, because you won't know ahead of time which ones will be right for you. If you are not satisfied with the first group you join, don't get discouraged; just move on to other organizations until you find the right one for you. Sooner or later, you will connect with compatible people and feel fulfilled. Stay connected with your family as they mature and change, because they are your most basic social network. Dedicating time and energy to developing and maintaining social relationships will pay dividends by extending your life and enhancing your mental and physical health. Focus on more than work; devote time and energy to building friendships and maintaining connections with friends and neighbors. Even if you work two jobs to make ends meet, social health is so vital that you must spend time building and maintaining relationships to live a long healthy life. It can be difficult to develop and maintain social relationships. Some individuals are naturally gregarious and love to meet new people, while others are shy and find it hard to connect with others. Developing new social relationships and nurturing existing social connections takes time and energy, so it helps to set goals about your social relationships the same way you have goals in your career. Social connections are important to living a long healthy life, so set goals and work hard to achieve them.

Relationship Goals. Most people have career goals, such as a promotion, a higher salary, or additional health benefits, and strive to attain them. Why not set similar goals to achieve good social health? Imagine what you would like your social life to be in five or ten years. Do you want to be married, make a new best friend, or join an interesting group? Do you want more friends, or would you like to reconnect with a family member you rarely see? To make that happen, set specific goals, schedule time to achieve them, and maintain these new relationships once they are established. Take time to connect with an old friend or someone new. Send a family member an email, call a friend when you have a few minutes, and schedule lunch with a coworker or family member to support your social health. To compensate for the time and effort you spend making new social connections, limit your television viewing and devote the extra time to making new relationships. Maintaining social connections should be a top priority if you want to live a long happy life. Connecting with others is like exercise—to reap the benefits, you need to do it every day. A good way to make new friends is to volunteer time to an organization in your community you care about. Another way to make new friends is to connect with people in a significant way rather than just saying "hello" or asking, "how are you?" To make a close connection with someone, ask them a significant question rather than simply offering a superficial greeting such as "how are you?" Talk to a stranger about something important, such as a risk they took in the past that worked well for them, ask about someone who was important in their life, or discuss the most meaningful gift they ever received.

To foster social health, interact honestly and meaningfully with others, say "thank you" sincerely, and do something to help others every week. When you receive an invitation to a party, pay particular attention to how you feel about attending. Are you delighted, neutral, or negative? Being mindful of how you feel will help you choose the right people as friends and make you feel better about yourself because you will enjoy being around people you love. Sometimes it's impossible to avoid a social gathering: business events are often obligatory, and you have to attend because that's what is expected as part of your job. Go to these functions with the attitude that you want to make a new friend rather than just attending and getting through the event as best you can. Practice making connections with others because it will improve your social skills and make meeting others easier. There are many ways to make new social connections.

How to Make Friends. There are many ways to make new friends. Have lunch with a coworker, introduce yourself to a stranger when you have the chance, be curious about new people you meet, and avoid being critical of yourself or others. If you move to a new city, the people there may connect in new and different ways, so be sensitive to their expectations and adopt the social procedures appropriate to your location. Being aware of local customs will make it easier to connect with new people. Be friendly and outgoing when you meet someone for the first time. Make the first overture so you start off on the right foot, and you will be surprised how easy it is to make a new social connection. To meet new people in a community, say "hello" when you first see them and be friendly. Another way to make new friends is to create a shared space in your neighborhood and establish a common goal, such as planting and maintaining a neighborhood garden or building a picnic table for public use. Invite your neighbors to join you in the project and see who shows up. Improve your neighborhood by planting a lawn in a vacant lot, cleaning up a local park, or painting a community fence. Feeling alone is a common problem in the busy modern world because more people live alone today than ever before. Moreover, the structure of a neighborhood or building can also influence how cohesive a neighborhood becomes and how isolated people feel in their surroundings. Architects, civil engineers, and urban planners try to create new communities with the goal of making them conducive to forming good social connections. Studies show that having parks in a neighborhood reduces people's sense of loneliness. However, if someone lives alone, they are more likely to feel isolated and depressed than individuals who has a large family and several friends.

According to the United States Census Bureau, the number of single person households increased between 1940 and 2020 from around 8 percent to almost 30 percent of the population. This means there are over 20 percent more people in America today who live alone than in earlier generations. Living alone doesn't necessarily mean a person is lonely or depressed, but not having other people around increases the likelihood of feeling isolated and sad. In addition to developing connections in your community, you can make friends at work or online.

Connecting at Work. On average, Americans spend approximately 90,000 hours working over their lifetimes. The workplace offers an excellent opportunity to make new friends and develop social connections. Moreover, making friends at work will improve your job satisfaction and productivity. Gallup asked whether people had a best friend at work and found one in three said "yes." Those individuals with friends at work were more productive, engaged in their work, and more positive about their jobs than those without close friends at work. Individuals who feel lonely on the job cost their employers more than four thousand dollars annually in sick days and lower productivity. Lonely workers are more likely to look for a new job, causing workplace disruption when they leave and creating additional costs for their employer to replace them. Social connections at work foster productivity and reduce turnover. However, only half of employees believe social connections are important for their career success and mental health. To build relationships at work, introduce yourself to a new employee when they join the company and invite them to lunch with your team. However, don't rely on co-workers alone for social connections. Develop a diverse pool of relationships that includes family, friends, neighbors, and co-workers. Having a variety of social connections gives you a robust social life and avoids becoming dependent on one set of people for your social, mental, and physical health. Another source of social connections is the people you meet online.

Connecting Online. Most of us spend time on the internet every day. Using social media correctly can generate healthy social connections and enhance our mental health. Making and maintaining satisfying social relationships online requires you to connect with others in a meaningful way through social media. If you use the internet to avoid social interactions, you will feel lonelier and miss opportunities to connect with people. There are two types of individuals who use the internet: those who regard social media as a means of making connections with others and people who use the internet as a substitute for social relationships. Those who use social media to connect with others report good mental health, while those who don't connect with others on the internet report poor mental and physical health. Using social media to develop new connections allows people to use the internet effectively without becoming dependent on it. On the other hand, if individuals use social media to escape personal connections, they will become dependent on escaping into what seems to be social relationships but is nothing but voyeurism. To evaluate how you use the internet, ask yourself how much time you spend searching for specific information or interacting meaningfully with others on social media, and how much time you spend simply watching something interesting on a social platform. Spending time intentionally on the internet and interacting with others is productive and satisfying, while searching for something interesting on social media may be unhealthy because you could be avoiding life by escaping into the internet.

Learning how to make and maintain social connections usually happens in childhood, but it can be acquired at any age if a person takes the time and effort to make new friends. Children and adolescents who feel socially connected at home are less likely to experience problems in school, such as depression, substance abuse, violence, or acquire sexually transmitted diseases. The opposite is also true; individuals who feel lonely at home are more likely to be depressed, antisocial, and isolated at school. Moreover, individuals who feel connected at home are more likely to be married at age fifty, while those who are isolated and lonely at home are more likely to be single adults. Parents and grandparents are responsible for helping children develop healthy relationships in the family, at school, and in life. Whether you are a parent, grandparent, uncle, or aunt, the time you spend with your children, grandchildren, nephews and nieces will leave an indelible mark on them. If you show them love and support, they will flourish, but if you ignore or criticize them, they will withdraw and fear social relationships. Social connections are a neglected part of living longer. Many people know that a good diet, daily exercise, and a healthy environment increase longevity, but few individuals are aware that developing and maintaining social relationships are an essential part of living a long healthy life.

Summary. Developing social relationships increases longevity by lowering the risk of a heart attack, developing Type 2 diabetes, developing depression, or developing Alzheimer's. However, opportunities for making social connections have declined in recent years, so modern adults spend more time alone and have fewer friends than earlier generations. Having friends, family, and a romantic partner increases longevity. Men with few social relationships are twice as likely to die young compared with those who have many social connections, and being alone is even more harmful for women. Social isolation among women makes them three times more likely to die over the following decade. The number and quality of social relationships needed for mental and physical health vary among individuals. Some people need many social connections to avoid being lonely, while others are happy with just a few close friends. Being a member of a group enhances physical, mental, and social health. However, many casual acquaintances are usually not adequate to maintain good mental health, because the quality of one's social connections is more important than the number. The need for social connections evolves, and there are many ways to make friends and achieve mental and physical health. Scientists measure social health by counting the number of satisfying relationships a person has with family, friends, a romantic partner, co-workers, and neighbors. However, some individuals are abrasive, toxic, or destructive, and should be avoided because they reduce life expectancy.

Being in a romantic relationship is important for mental and physical health, but a strong partnership alone won't guarantee it. Maintain family relationships, develop close social connections with friends, and become part of a community to increase longevity. Get involved in a group such as a church, cooking class, book club, or bridge group to stay connected and live longer. Dedicating time and energy to relationships will pay dividends by extending longevity and maintaining mental and physical health. Building new relationships and nurturing existing social connections takes time and energy, so you need to set goals to achieve social health, just as you do in your career. There are several ways to make connections, such as having lunch with a friend or introducing yourself to a stranger. To meet people in a new community, begin by saying "hello." Another way to make friends is to create a shared space in your new neighborhood and set a common goal, such as planting and maintaining a neighborhood garden or building a picnic table. The number of single-person households in America increased from around 8 percent of the population in 1940 to almost 30 percent in 2020. Architects, civil engineers, and urban planners are designing new communities to foster social connections. For example, studies show that having parks in a neighborhood reduces people's sense of loneliness. In addition to developing connections in your community, you can make friends at work or online. Whether you are a parent, grandparent, uncle, or aunt, the time you spend with your children, grandchildren, nephews, and nieces will leave an indelible mark on them. If you show them love and support, they will flourish, but if you ignore or criticize them, they will withdraw and fear social connections. Developing and maintaining social relationships are not recognized as part of living longer.

8

WORK AND LONGEVITY

Baby Boomers are living longer and retiring later than earlier generations. Studies show that working longer is associated with increased longevity and better physical health, although the specific effects depend on the person and the job. Research shows that working longer is associated with better mental and physical health because a career provides employees with a sense of purpose. Continuing to work also avoids feelings of isolation, promotes financial security, and lowers stress among older workers. However, if a job requires hard physical labor, causes prolonged stress, or creates low job satisfaction, working longer can reduce longevity. Some supervisors view older workers as professionals with a lifetime of experience, while others believe employees should retire at age 65 because older workers are more expensive and difficult to manage. What do managers mean by the term "older worker?" Does working past age sixty-five mean an employee is old? Or should managers recognize that chronological age may not be an accurate measure of worker competence compared with the psychological and physical characteristics of each individual? Some fifty-year-old workers are ready to retire, while other seventy-year-old employees are still engaged in their job and bring energy, talent, and experience to the workplace.

Modern business depends on technology, so leveraging the skills older workers have acquired makes good sense. Why waste talent because an employee is approaching the arbitrary retirement age of sixty-five? Many managers believe assessing each individual in terms of his or her psychological age rather than rigidly pushing employees to retire when they reach sixty-five is good management practice. However, other employers believe requiring workers to retire at sixty-five is the best policy, because they believe older individuals are slowing down and lack the motivation and ability to be productive. A minority of supervisors think older workers are looking forward to retirement, becoming disengaged, and losing interest in their jobs, which is why they want them to retire at 65. However, many older workers feel their employers have given up on them and don't respect their contributions to the company. Who is right?

Managers who are clear about priorities, give reliable feedback to their employees, and offer opportunities for advancement to all workers, no matter their age, can keep older workers engaged and productive, while supervisors who send mixed messages to older employees, supply ambiguous feedback to people nearing retirement, and stifle opportunities for advancement after employees reach age fifty-five, generate indifferent older employees. Studies suggest that workers stay engaged in their jobs based on three factors: believing they have autonomy at work, gaining mastery of tasks, and feeling a sense of purpose from their work. Employees who have control over their time and are assigned work they can do feel they have a purpose within the company, stay engaged, and remain productive.

Autonomy. The relationships between employer and employee are changing. No longer can a supervisor require workers to do a particular job in a certain way. Today, companies use robots to perform simple, repetitive tasks that were once performed by unskilled laborers in earlier generations. Consequently, managers assign more complex tasks to experienced employees who know their jobs and allow them to manage them their own way. This is what human resource experts mean when they advise supervisors to give experienced employees autonomy. Modern managers can no longer exercise strict control over talented workers because new technologies such as artificial intelligence (AI) are shifting the relationship between supervisors and workers. Change is constant, so employers and employees must adjust to the differing demands of the modern workplace. Because individuals are living longer, many older workers expect to stay engaged in their careers, continue being productive, and feeling good about themselves into advanced age. Talented workers believe being forced to retire at age sixty-five wastes talent and disrupts business. Planning for evolving work requirements and the needs of older workers can benefit a corporation, as change is constant.

Change and work. There are two types of workplace changes: some are gradual and unfold over generations, while others are rapid and materialize quickly. It took generations for the United States to evolve from an agrarian nation to a modern industrial society where most people were engaged in manufacturing rather than farming, but in the last forty years, many jobs have changed from work demanding physical labor to office tasks which can be done by both men and women. More recently, many American companies have shifted from manufacturing things to producing services. Rapid workplace changes usually require the adoption of new technologies, such as computers, which enhance worker efficiency and productivity but require complex skills to operate.

Also, more people are working remotely due to the COVID-19 pandemic and changing attitudes about how companies structure their workplace. Technological changes require managers and employees to acquire new skills. Although the workplace changes constantly, it follows predictable patterns that allow business owners and supervisors to anticipate and manage innovation.

Patterns of Change. During the early stages of a business revolution, employers often hire outside experts to study the company and supply information needed to guide management as they adjust to evolving challenges. New ideas are needed to understand and deal with shifting business demands. In the early stages of a business change, goals are vague, but as the change progresses, they become more focused on a few new ideas and techniques. However, even when the requirements for change become clear to management, adopting advanced technology to address these challenges does not occur until an external event forces management to change. Examples of external factors that can force a corporation to adopt new technology include recessions, inflation, shifts in consumer demand, increased competition, political or social forces, mergers and acquisitions, regulatory changes, and wars. When a major business revolution occurs, recruiting employees with the skills and knowledge to manage new job requirements becomes more difficult because supervisors don't always know which skills are required to address these challenges. What factors force management to change how it manages its employees?

Factors that drive change in the workplace include mergers or acquisitions, because new management structures and cultures must be accommodated, different workers and managers must be integrated, and a new CEO may shift the goals and expectations of a company and increase the need for autonomy and flexibility among employees, creating rapid changes in employment demands. Modern businesses place more emphasis on knowledge and demand less physical strength than earlier companies. A significant factor driving today's changes is machine intelligence, which is altering the control people have over their careers as new skills and types of information are required for modern jobs. Change driven by artificial intelligence and automation is shifting the skills companies require and revising which types of employees managers value. These workplace changes have created more temporary jobs, part-time employment, faster technological change, and greater uncertainty among managers and workers. The Industrial Revolution that began in England during the middle of the eighteenth century shifted work from households to factories. Still, recent technological changes have created new skill demands as American corporations shifted from manufacturing to service industries, allowing more women to enter the workforce and changing social expectations for supervisors. The introduction of artificial intelligence has also heightened employees' concerns that they will be replaced by machines and lose their jobs.

Technological Threats. Technical advances have often eliminated jobs and required employees to acquire new skills to remain employable, but the creative destruction caused by the introduction of artificial intelligence has sparked fear among white-collar workers who worry an intelligent machine will replace them. As a result, older workers are thinking more about work-life balance, seeking greater control over their careers, and striking out on their own as freelancers rather than staying employed by a company. Surveys of modern workers show they want more control over when and how they work, what they do, how long they work, and for whom. Older workers feel they have given companies the best years of their lives and deserve time to pursue their own interests as they near retirement. At the same time, older employees face increasing demands to care for their aging parents while having responsibilities for children or grandchildren.

Today, older workers feel the need to pay more attention to their personal goals, such as spending time with their family, caring for aging parents, or traveling, rather than placing their career first. Because people are living longer, many older employees say they intend to work an extra decade before they retire to build savings. Because employees are choosing to work longer, they need continuing education to maintain professional competence. During a change, employers often respond to uncertainty by hiring part-time workers, outsourcing tasks to independent contractors, and delaying hiring until they understand the skills needed to manage the challenges. Moreover, older workers are leaving company employment, establishing their own consulting businesses, and contacting with corporations to perform jobs as needed. What are the advantages and disadvantages of this development in the workplace and is the change good for employees and companies?

Independent Contractors. Studies show that many older workers prefer to leave company employment for freelance work, because it gives them more control of their time and life. Over twenty percent of current jobs are performed by independent contractors rather than corporate employees. If current trends continue, in another generation, freelance workers may outnumber corporate employees because they offer flexibility and lower costs to corporations. One concern among human resource experts is that independent contracting is less secure than corporate employment, so employees who choose to freelance may need to build additional capital to tide them over slow periods. Uncertain employment can also affect employees' mental and physical health. To reduce uncertainty, some independent contractors are hiring agents to market themselves to corporations and ensure they have enough work to stay solvent and thrive. Because Americans are living longer and retiring later, this is creating challenges for managers.

About 20 percent of Americans aged sixty-five or older are still working, which is a significant increase from earlier generations. The problems associated with older workers retiring later is that managers may view them as outdated, expensive, and set in their ways, rather than experienced, reliable and well-trained employees. To meet this challenge, older workers need to convince their managers they are valuable to the corporation. Older workers must maintain and enhance their skills by taking advanced training, develop the competences needed by modern employers, and remain flexible, so they are seen as a company asset, appreciated, respected, and retained rather than forced to retire. If older workers allow their skills to atrophy and don't keep up with newer technologies, they will be seen by their company as a liability and forced out if they don't retire. Older workers who maintain and enhance their skills are valuable to a company because they have accumulated institutional memories and traditions which will be lost if they are forced to retire at age sixty-five. However, to remain attractive to employers, older workers must maintain their competence and acquire new technical knowledge to remain employable in a changing marketplace. New technologies shift the skills required by companies, so employees need to engage in lifelong learning to acquire the skills needed in today's workplace. Another reason to retain older employees is that they have developed important skills such as leadership, reliability, and initiative that are valuable to a corporation. However, some managers have biases against older workers.

Corporate Myths. Several corporate myths work against retaining older workers, including the belief that mature workers cost more than younger employees, older workers don't have up-to-date skills, training older workers is more expensive, they are less productive than younger workers, and older employees are difficult to manage.

Are Older Workers More Expensive? Many managers believe that because older workers earn higher salaries than younger workers, they cost the company more and should be retired at age sixty-five. However, older workers have more experience, a broader range of skills, and as a result, may be more productive than younger workers, so their actual cost may be less than a younger worker when increased productivity is factored into the mix. In addition, replacing an experienced older worker is costly compared with keeping him or her employed. Hiring and training a new worker costs around 90 percent of the new employee's first-year wage, so replacing an older worker may not be cost-effective. Moreover, older workers take off less time than younger workers because they don't have children to care for and suffer fewer workplace injuries because they have learned how to minimize risks around the machines they are operating. Finally, older workers are punctual, dependable, and less likely to resign or move to another company compared with younger workers. So, why do many companies still retire employees at sixty-five? Because some managers believe older workers don't maintain or update their skills.

Does Retraining Older Workers Waste Money? Studies show that older workers can learn new skills and often transfer knowledge from one task to another. Continuing education can boost productivity among older workers, keep them engaged in their jobs, and help the corporation retain experienced employees. Some older workers resist learning new skills, and should be encouraged to retire. Still, many mature employees welcome the opportunity to gain new experience, acquire valuable skills, and advance in their careers. If an older worker is willing to learn, he or she should be allowed to increase their value to the corporation. Often, older workers know how to teach themselves new skills, and that ability can be invaluable to a company. Finally, many older workers are naturally curious and seek out new opportunities. Some supervisors believe older workers are slowing down and not so productive as eager young employees. Are they right?

Are Older Workers Less Productive? Some older workers have not maintained their skills and, as a result, are falling behind younger employees. However, many older workers have skills that make them more productive than younger workers; they can mentor younger employees and are better at decision-making than new hires. A review of research showed that around 40 percent of the time there was no difference in productivity between older and younger workers, about 30 percent of the time younger workers were more productive, and 28 percent of the time older workers were more productive than younger workers. This review concluded that there is no significant difference in productivity between older and younger workers. However, some supervisors still believe mature workers should retire at sixty-five because they are difficult to manage.

Are Older Workers Hard to Manage? Supervising older workers can be challenging, especially if they are mature and have more experience than young supervisors. Because many American workers are postponing retirement, managing older employees is becoming a pressing issue in many companies. The key to managing older workers is to respect them, avoid stereotyping, and not assume they have less energy, are set in their ways, or are unmotivated. Managers need to communicate with older workers to understand the mature employee's attitude and become comfortable managing them. Moreover, supervisors should listen to their older employees, because they have valuable experience that can help solve difficult problems. Older employees can also mentor younger workers, taking some of that burden from managers. Older workers often have better work habits compared with younger workers, are more dependable, and take fewer days off. Older workers also have leadership skills that can be valuable on a team. They make good role models and are generally more loyal to the company than younger workers, as they have a long history with the business. Keeping older workers can be a competitive advantage for a corporation because they have experience, are loyal, can mentor younger workers, and are just as productive as younger employees.

Summary. Americans are living and working longer today, which is creating new challenges for corporate managers. How should supervisors deal with older workers? Are workers old at sixty-five? Or should managers recognize that chronological age is not so crucial as psychological age? Some older workers are ready to retire, while others bring experience, competence, and maturity to the workplace. Taking advantage of the skills older workers possess is good for business. Why waste talent because an employee turns sixty-five? Doesn't it make sense to assess each individual in terms of his or her psychological age? Managers often believe older workers are not engaged in their work, have lost interest in their job, and want to retire. However, many older workers want to continue working because they love their job and don't want to retire. Studies show that employees who have control of their work, know how to do their job, and have a sense of purpose, want to continue working, and are good employees.

9

MONEY AND AGING

Studies show that individuals with high incomes or who inherit wealth live longer than those with low incomes. The rich have access to better health care, eat a healthier diet, and reside in safer neighborhoods that offer clean water and air. Having more money also gives rich individuals access to advice about preventive medical care and the benefits of advanced medical technologies compared with poor people. Wealthier individuals can afford to live in communities with green spaces that lower stress and contribute to longevity. Having a high income or inherited wealth also limits financial stress, which reduces mortality. Being wealthy allows people to pursue more education which promotes healthy habits and encourages better lifestyle choices. Moreover, the gap in life expectancy between rich and poor has been widening in recent decades, meaning that today wealthier individuals live even longer than their poorer peers did in earlier times. The richest one percent of modern men lives fourteen years longer on average than the poorest one percent, and the richest one percent of modern women lives over ten years longer on average compared with the poorest one percent. Scientists have studied how higher income and inherited wealth contribute to longevity and have found that the relationship is complex.

Research on Wealth and Longevity. A 2016 study explored the relationship between income and longevity across over a billion people, estimating life expectancy at age 40 separately by sex and geographic area. This research yielded four conclusions: first, higher income is associated with greater longevity across the entire range of income and wealth; second, the difference in longevity between rich and poor increased more than two years for men and nearly three years for women between 1999 and 2014; third, the results produced a nearly linear relationship between the log of mortality rate and age for Americans across all levels of income. This result suggests that there is no threshold for the effect of money on longevity, but it takes much more money to increase longevity at higher wealth levels; finally, the study found that the difference between how many years men and women live, decreases with age. Among Americans aged twenty, the difference in predicted longevity of men and women was approximately five years; at age fifty, the difference in predicted longevity between men and women was around three years; at age eighty the predicted difference in longevity between men and women was two-and-one-half years; and at age one hundred, the predicted difference in longevity between men and women was only approximately one-and-one -half years. At all ages, women lived longer than men. Smaller gains in life expectancy occur at higher income levels, while the most significant longevity gains from higher income occur among people earning between $10,000 and $30,000. Above $100,000, there is little additional gain in longevity as family income and wealth increase. In addition to income, where people live also affects their longevity.

Residential Area and Longevity. Significant differences in longevity occurred among populations living in New York, San Francisco, Dallas, and Detroit, especially among families with annual incomes below $30,000. Results showed that individuals who earned incomes below thirty thousand dollars and lived in New York survived approximately one year longer on average than similar residents in San Francisco, who lived about one year longer on average than residents in Dallas, who lived almost two years longer on average than residents in Detroit. Poor residents of Detroit had the lowest average life expectancy among these four regional groups. The results were nearly identical for men and women, with females again living longer than males. Nevada, Indiana, and Oklahoma had the lowest average life expectancies in America, while New York, California, and Vermont had the highest. Hawaii, Maine, and Massachusetts had the most significant gains in longevity between 2001 and 2014. There are also several factors that shorten the lifespan of the poor.

Life expectancy is negatively correlated with smoking ($r = -0.69$), and obesity ($r = -0.47$), but positively correlated with exercise ($r = 0.32$). Access to health insurance is not associated with longevity, because individuals who have health insurance don't live longer than those without it. Attending church does not affect life expectancy, but home values are positively correlated with living longer ($r = 0.72$). Longevity is also positively correlated with local government expenditures ($r = 0.57$), population density ($r = 0.48$), and percentage of college graduates in the community ($r = 0.42$). These results suggest that communities which spend more on the welfare of their citizens, especially if they are cities with dense populations that include many college graduates, live longer. The relationship between income and longevity is a continuous function, according to this study, meaning that across the entire range of income and wealth in the United States, wealthier individuals live longer than the poor. Finally, the study showed that having more money increases life expectancy for both rich and poor up to approximately one hundred thousand dollars in annual income and has only a small effect at higher income levels.

Between 2001 and 2014, average life expectancy of Americans increased as income rose. However, Americans in the top one percent of income gained around an average of three years of longevity during this interval, while those in the bottom one percent of income gained little extra longevity. Variations in life expectancy within the different geographical areas was associated with differences in rates of smoking, obesity, and exercise among rich and poor. Poor people smoke more, exercise less, and gain more weight than rich individuals, and as a result the poor live shorter lives on average compared with the wealthy. There was no increase in longevity among poor individuals after they became eligible for Medicare at age sixty-five, suggesting that access to medical care was not a significant factor affecting the association between income and longevity in the United States between 2001 and 2014. One surprising finding was that low-income individuals who live in high-income areas live longer on average than low-income people who live in poor areas. The researchers speculated that poor individuals who live in high income areas may be influenced by the healthy behavior of wealthy people around them or are forced to smoke less because of local laws. Alternatively, it may be that most of the poor people living in wealthy areas are foreign-born citizens who generally live longer on average than native-born Americans. As you probably expect, poverty decreases life expectancy.

Poverty and Longevity. In 2024, scientists examined mortality rates among approximately 86,000 adults living in 12 southeastern states. The results from this study showed a strong negative association between income and mortality, with the very high death rates occurring among families with an annual income below fifteen thousand dollars. In this study, poor white Americans experienced higher average mortality rates than poor Black Americans, contrary to findings from other studies that show Black Americans in general die younger than white Americans. This means that being very poor is especially damaging to white Americans. In this study, average life expectancy was more than ten years higher for individuals in the top income group than for those in the bottom income group. However, average life expectancy can be increased for rich and poor alike by following a healthy lifestyle that includes not smoking or drinking excessive alcohol, eating a healthy diet that includes vegetables and fruits, avoiding processed foods that contain excess salt and chemicals, or sweet drinks with lots of sugar, and exercising regularly. The reasons poor Americans die younger than their wealthier peers include having limited access to health care, not getting physical examinations, being too poor to afford medication or diagnostic tests, and living far away from physicians' offices, clinics, or hospitals. Moreover, poor people generally consume an unhealthy diet high in salt, sugar, and saturated fats.

As a result, the poor suffer from nutritional deficiencies, obesity, and poor physical health. People living in poverty lack access to clean water, air, and a safe environment, which can cause respiratory diseases and early death. Also, poor individuals who live in crowded conditions suffer more from the spread of communicative diseases because there are more people living in a small confined space. Financial problems cause stress, which has a negative effect on longevity. Poverty also limits access to education, restricts lifestyle choices, and lowers longevity. Research in Virginia found that a city with a median family income of $124,000 had an average life expectancy of over 80 years, while another city with a median income of $48,000 had an average life expectancy of only 71 years. Individuals living in poverty also die more frequently from suicide and alcohol-related diseases compared with persons living in wealthy areas. Since having a high income or inherited wealth is associated with living longer, what rules should people follow to become wealthy and live a long healthy life?

Money Management. Wealth management strategies can help a person become wealthier. The first step is to get a good education, because no one can take that away from you, knowledge enriches life and leads to better jobs and higher earnings. Second, when searching for investment ideas, look for securities that generate cash flow through dividends or interest payments, because income from investments is a reliable way to become wealthy. Third, look for unique opportunities to invest in companies or situations that will grow your wealth over time. Fourth, diversify your investments among stocks, bonds, real estate, and money market funds, so that if the value of one asset falls, you won't lose most of your money. Begin saving and investing as soon as you start working, because the longer you grow your nest egg, the wealthier you will become, since compounding grows wealth and the longer you have before you begin spending your savings (because your earn income on the interest, dividends, and appreciation you have accumulated, which grows your money at a faster rate) the more money you will accumulate. Finally, be skeptical of investments that look too good to be true, because they usually are. Don't be fooled by claims of guaranteed high returns, because past performance is no assurance of similar results in the future. Perform due diligence on every security you consider, research the background of your investment advisor, talk to a lawyer about your investment plans, and invest for the long term rather than trying to get rich quick. A fundamental requirement of investing is to know your risk tolerance and avoid buying securities that are too volatile. Try to avoid losing principal, because it's difficult to make up a huge loss. Don't speculate by investing in risky securities.

Keep your Money Safe. Minimizing risk is one of the most important rules of sound investing. Never ignore red flags just because an investment looks too good to miss and won't be around for long; because there are always other opportunities available, and you should never rush into an investment because the seller claims it will be gone soon. Trust facts and logic rather than personal feelings. A good investment rule is to assume that every security you are considering may be a scam, because being skeptical will help you avoid putting money into risky assets. Every investor should diversify, so he or she doesn't put all their money in a single security that can lose most of its value. There are four classes of assets every investor should consider having in his or her portfolio: investment grade bonds, stocks issued by major corporations, well-located real estate, and money market funds. Over the long run, the performance of these four assets is not highly correlated, which means that when one asset falls in value, the others don't generally follow suit, causing you to lose most of your money. Investment advisers suggest that young investors should place more of their wealth in stocks and real estate, because these investments historically have produced higher returns in the long run but carry more risk of loss than government bonds or money market funds. Investing in riskier assets when you are young is a smart strategy, because securities such as stocks or real estate generally produce a higher return over time compared with bonds or money market funds, and you have longer to recover from a loss when you are young. As you mature, financial advisors recommend allocating less of your portfolio to stocks and real estate and investing more funds in bonds and money market funds that are less volatile and more liquid. What are some ways an investor can reduce risk in his or her portfolio?

Dealing With Risk. The first thing an investor should do is evaluate his or her risk tolerance, which reflects how a person feels about gains and losses in a portfolio. Suppose an investor has low risk tolerance (meaning he or she is more concerned about losing money than increasing wealth). In that case, that person should invest in conservative assets such as money market funds, bonds, and real estate. On the other hand, if an investor has a high tolerance for risk, (meaning he or she is more interested in gaining money rather than worried about losing money) this investor should place more assets in the stock market, because over the long run, stocks are likely to produce higher returns than bonds and money market funds. Knowing your individual risk tolerance will guide you toward investing in assets that are appropriate for your emotions, age, and stage of life. Moreover, investing in assets that align with your risk tolerance will help you stay invested over the long haul, which is essential if you want to become wealthy. Risk is associated with volatility, and securities that generate high volatility can cause significant losses. Stocks and real estate are more volatile and therefore riskier than bonds or money market funds, but they tend to generate higher returns over the long run.

The path to sound investing is to balance your investment goals against your tolerance for risk and allocate your assets accordingly. If you are older or risk-averse, you should invest more of your money in bonds and money market funds, while if you are young or risk-tolerant, you should allocate more money to stocks and real estate. There are five types of risk: market risk, inflation risk, liquidity risk, currency risk, and interest rate risk. Market risk means that the value of stocks, bonds, or real estate may go down; inflation risk refers to the possibility that all prices will raise and your assets will be worth less in dollar terms; liquidity risk refers to the possibility that you can't sell an asset when you need the money for an emergency; currency risk happens when you invest in foreign securities, and your investments are exposed to fluctuations in the value of your assets valued in another currency relative to dollars; and interest rate risk means that when interest rates rise, the value of bonds goes down. Which assets are exposed to the different types of investment risk? Stocks have higher market risk than bonds because stocks are more volatile. Bonds and money market funds lose value when inflation is high, because they earn low rates of interest, and their value falls when prices go up. In contrast, stocks, real estate, and inflation-protected treasury bonds are generally safe hedges against inflation.

Money market funds, stocks, and treasury or corporate bonds have low liquidity risk, while real estate is more difficult to sell quickly at a fair price. To avoid currency risk, invest in American securities or dollar-denominated stocks and bonds issued by foreign companies. To reduce interest rate risk, buy stocks, real estate, or gold because these assets generally appreciate when the Federal Reserve raises interest rates. When interest rates rise, bonds lose value. To reduce portfolio risk, learn all you can about the asset you are considering buying, pay attention to market conditions, and study Federal Reserve policy. For example, does the Fed intend to stimulate the economy by lowering interest rates because it fears a recession, or does it intend to restrict monetary policy by raising interest rates because inflation is growing? Every investment class has unique risks and rewards. For example, if you buy mortgage-backed securities, make sure the value of the collateral property associated with the security is around two times the value of the mortgage, and confirm that you are first in line to recover your capital if the property goes into foreclosure. If you invest in a managed security fund, investigate the past performance of the agent who is managing the fund you are considering to make certain he or she has a long positive record of performance before you invest. Finally, read about how to invest and follow the advice of investment experts. One of the most sophisticated and intelligent financial experts of modern times was Benjamin Graham, and it pays to follow his advice when you are analyzing potential investments.

Benjamin Graham on Investing. Warren Buffett, widely regarded as one of the wisest investors who ever lived, recommends following Benjamin Graham's advice when analyzing and investing in securities. Graham believed investors should avoid speculating and focus on investing their money in assets that promise the safety of principal and an adequate return on investment. If an asset is risky and does not produce an adequate return, then, according to Graham, it is a speculative security and should be avoided. He recommended taking a defensive approach to investing and avoiding buying stocks or other volatile assets with borrowed money. Graham also believed investors should buy assets that are appropriate for their stage of life, lifestyle, personal needs, financial goals, and family situation. He warned that investors should always consider the risk posed by inflation when they are investing. Graham warned that if the United States government is printing money or keeping interest rates abnormally low to stimulate the economy, the value of the dollar will fall, inflation will rise, and the prudent investor should sell money market funds or bonds and buy stocks, real estate, gold, or inflation-protected treasury bonds to avoid losing purchasing power.

Graham also recommended that the defensive investor buy corporate stocks and bonds, allocate more money to stocks than to bonds when they are young, and allocate more to bonds as they mature. That way, Graham believed the prudent investor would maximize returns when young and enjoy the safety, liquidity, and assured income of bonds and money market funds in retirement. He also believed that investors should be cautious when selecting assets for their portfolio. Graham emphasized what he called "the margin of safety" when buying assets. He advocated investing in securities with a proven record of paying dividends and buying safe bonds, such as United States Treasury securities or investment-grade corporate bonds. Graham believed that paying a fair price for high-quality securities was a safer investment strategy than trying to buy low-grade stocks or bonds at a discount. He also recommended that investors buy a diversified portfolio of stocks, bonds, real estate, and money market funds to avoid huge losses in a single asset. Graham also suggested that investors approach their investments in a businesslike manner and take responsibility for their own decisions rather than delegating portfolio management to a professional agent. Another Graham rule was never to make an investment that didn't produce a fair return on capital by paying interest or dividends. Finally, he recommended that individuals believe in themselves and stick with their strategy in the long run rather than trying to get rich quickly.

Summary. Rich people live longer than the poor because they have access to better health care, eat a healthy diet, and reside in safe, desirable neighborhoods that offer clean water and air. High income or inherited wealth allows rich people access to more education, which encourages better lifestyle choices. The gap in life expectancy between rich and poor has been growing in recent decades, so today the wealthiest one percent of men live fourteen years longer on average than the poorest one percent of men, and the wealthiest one percent of women live over ten years longer on average compared with the poorest one percent of women. A 2016 study explored the relationship between income and longevity across over a billion people, estimating life expectancy at age 40 separately by sex and geographic area. The researchers concluded that higher income is associated with greater longevity across the entire range of income and wealth, the difference in longevity between rich and poor increased more than two years for men and nearly three years for women between 1999 and 2014, and they found nearly a linear relationship between the log of mortality rate and age for Americans across the entire range of income from the highest to lowest percentiles. These researchers also discovered that the difference in longevity between men and women decreases as they age. Among Americans aged twenty, the difference in predicted longevity of men and women is approximately five years; at age fifty, the difference in longevity between men and women is around three years; at age eighty, the difference in longevity between men and women is two-and-one-half years; and at age one hundred, the difference in longevity between men and women is approximately one-and-one-half years. However, at all ages, women live longer than men.

Where you reside also affects how long you live. Studies have found significant differences in longevity among populations living in New York, San Francisco, Dallas, and Detroit, especially among families with incomes below $30,000. Citizens of Nevada, Indiana, and Oklahoma had the lowest average life expectancies in America, while those living in New York, California, and Vermont had the highest. Hawaii, Maine, and Massachusetts had the largest gains in longevity between 2001 and 2014. Life expectancy is negatively correlated with smoking rates (r = -0.69), and obesity (r = -0.47), but positively correlated with exercising (r = 0.32). However, individuals with health insurance don't live longer than those without. Life expectancy is positively correlated with longevity for individuals in the top quartile of income (r = 0.37). Home values are also positively correlated with living longer (r = 0.72), and residents of communities that spend more on welfare, especially if they are cities with dense populations that include many college graduates, tend to live longer.

Between 2001 and 2014, the average life expectancy of Americans increased as income rose. However, poor Americans die earlier than their wealthier peers because of limited access to health care, not having a physical examination, being too poor to afford medications or diagnostic tests, and living far from physicians' offices, clinics, or hospitals. Moreover, poor individuals consume an unhealthy diet high in salt, sugar, saturated fats, and processed foods. People living in poverty lack access to clean water and a safe environment, which can cause diseases. Also, poor individuals who live in crowded conditions suffer more from communicative diseases that rich individuals.

CONCLUSION

In the 1600s, English physicians began studying human life expectancy systematically to understand why some people live longer than others. They discovered that most of the increase in longevity happens because more infants and children survived childhood due to better public health procedures. Modern humans live longer due to better sanitation, vaccines, antibiotics, improved nutrition, vehicle safety regulations, and effective medical care. The three advances that contributed most to human longevity were the development of artificial fertilizers, the building of sewer systems, and the discovery of vaccines. Modern scientists have shown that a healthy lifestyle, satisfying social relations, purposeful work, and financial security also help humans live longer. The increase in human longevity began when John Snow, an English physician, plotted the distribution of cholera deaths in London and found they were concentrated around a single London water well. When the parish board agreed to remove the pump handle from that well the incidence of cholera deaths dropped dramatically, proving that cholera was caused by contaminated drinking water. After Snow's discovery, London authorities built a sewer system to separate human waste from drinking water, added chlorine to kill bacteria, and reduced the incidence of infectious diseases.

Another significant advance in public health was the discovery of pasteurization, which killed bacteria in wine, beer, and milk by heating. In the nineteenth century, half of children died before their fifth birthday because of infectious diseases caused by contaminated milk, impure foods, or air-borne diseases. However, pasteurization of milk was not required in America until 1915. German chemists discovered how to synthesize ammonium nitrate from atmospheric nitrogen in 1909, producing artificial fertilizer that helped farmers feed an expanding population. Before the discovery of artificial fertilizer, farmers spread animal waste on their fields, but it was in short supply and difficult to use. In the 1930s Thomas McKown, a British Canadian physician, found that the population of England had begun to increase years before physicians discovered effective cures for most illnesses, suggesting that something other than medical care was helping people live longer. He speculated that advances in public health, such as better sanitation, prevented epidemics and increased human lifespans. Another factor that increased life expectancy was auto safety. In the 1950s, auto accidents had become a significant cause of death in America. To reduce traffic accidents, stop lights were installed and speed limits set, but deaths from auto accidents continued to climb. In 1955, Ford Motor Company introduced lap belts, a padded dashboard, and a recessed steering wheel in their cars, but executives at General Motors believed highlighting auto accidents was a bad idea and did not support building and advertising safer cars. It was not until Ralph Nadar published his book, *Unsafe at Any Speed: The Designed in Dangers of the American Automobile* in 1965 that car buyers began demanding safer autos. In 1966, Congress created the United States Transportation Agency to study and recommend safety standards for automobiles. Modern scientists have found that several factors affect longevity.

Genetics, Environment, and Longevity. Public health experts have shown that aging is affected by genetics, the environment, disease, and metabolic processes. Advances in nutrition, sanitation, and medicine allow babies born today to live an average of 40 years longer than their ancient ancestors, who lived an average of about 35 years. The heritability of longevity is slightly higher among men ($r = 0.26$) than women ($r = 0.23$), and the heritability of living to be one hundred is also higher for men ($r = 0.48$) than women ($r = 0.33$). Children of parents who live to one hundred are seven times more likely to live a long healthy life compared with the general population. People who live to one hundred don't smoke, avoid becoming obese, exercise, eat a healthy diet, and deal effectively with stress, so they rarely develop high blood pressure, heart disease, cancer, or Type 2 diabetes. Scientists have studied groups of individuals who live in areas called Blue Zones to discover why they live longer than most humans.

People residing in Blue Zones often live to 100, while the average life expectancy in America is around 77 years. They have found Blue Zones in Sardinia, Italy; Okinawa, Japan; Loma Linda, California, among Seventh-day Adventists; Ikaria, Greece; and Nicoya, Costa Rica. Factors associated with living long and healthy lives in these Blue Zones include exercise, having a sense of purpose, minimizing stress, avoiding obesity, eating a Mediterranean diet, drinking alcohol in moderation, and maintaining close social relationships with family and friends. On the other hand, inherited diseases that run in families and are passed from one or both parents to their children decrease longevity. The six most common heritable genetic diseases are sickle cell anemia, cystic fibrosis, Tay-Sachs disease, hemophilia, Huntington's disease, and muscular dystrophy.

Hereditary Diseases. Sickle cell disease is caused by genes that encode for hemoglobin proteins. Individuals who develop sickle cell anemia produce abnormal blood cells that are rigid and shaped like a sickle rather than flexible and oval like normal blood cells. Cystic Fibrosis affects the production of mucus, sweat, and digestive juices. Children who suffer from this disease produce thick, sticky mucus that can damage their respiratory, digestive, and reproductive systems. Tay-Sachs disease is found among Eastern European Jews, French Canadian communities in Quebec, and within Cajun communities. It is caused by the lack of an enzyme that digests fats, allowing fatty substances to reach toxic levels in the brains of affected individuals. A juvenile form of Tay-Sachs disease can appear during childhood, and these individuals may survive into their teens. Another inherited disease is hemophilia, which produces internal bleeding. This disorder is more common in males and is caused by a deficiency in blood-clotting agents, producing excessive internal bleeding among affected individuals. Huntington's disease is a life-threatening disorder that appears in mid-life among individuals who inherit a defective gene. It causes progressive destruction of brain cells, leading to mental deterioration and loss of muscle function. In contrast, muscular dystrophy interferes with the production of proteins necessary for muscle development. This disorder occurs most often among boys and symptoms usually begin during childhood. There is no cure, but drugs can manage severe symptoms for a few years. Scientists have developed several theories of aging, but none has been proved to be a comprehensive explanation of the process.

Theories of Aging. Most theories of aging assume that after reproduction, there has been little evolutionary pressure to extend life, and that's why people age and die. Aging generally begins around forty, although there is wide variation in when aging occurs and how quickly it progresses. Aging is associated with a decline in the functioning of stem cells, and some scientists believe that process causes human aging. Another theory of aging is that free radicals accumulate in the human body. Aging may also be caused by toxic environmental factors which damage DNA. This theory is supported by studies showing that mutations can cause lethal genetic diseases. Although humans age in similar ways, life expectancy is not the same for all groups. Specifically, Black and Hispanic American men die younger than white men, and poor individuals die earlier than the rich. There seems to be an upper limit to how long humans can live, because the oldest documented woman lived to be one hundred twenty-two, and the longest-lived man was one hundred sixteen when he died. As you might expect, people who receive good medical care live longer.

Physical Exams and Longevity. Regular physical exams increase longevity by detecting serious problems early when there is a good chance of effective treatment. Primary care physicians offer physical examinations as part of their practice, and individuals who meet with a physician annually live significantly longer than those who don't. These physicians also offer cancer screening and early diagnosis of mental problems. A physical exam assesses current health, detects early signs of medical problems, and treats developing medical issues before they progress. Due to advances in nutrition, sanitation, and medicine, babies born today can expect to live an average of forty years longer than their ancient ancestors who survived an average of about thirty-five years. A good diet will also increase life expectancy.

Diet and Longevity. The Mediterranean diet includes low-fat cheese, salmon or sardines, fresh fruits and vegetables, legumes, whole grains, nuts, olive oil, and chicken. This diet reduces the risk of cancer, high blood pressure, heart disease, and strokes, while promoting weight loss and health. Lean meat such as roasted lamb or veal cutlets may be consumed occasionally. Still, red meat that contains marbled fat should be avoided because it can lead to weight gain, high blood pressure, stroke, heart disease, and is associated with some types of cancer. Other sources of healthy protein include low-fat cheese and yogurt which provide building blocks for muscles, calcium for strong bones, and probiotics to support gut health and general well-being. Almonds, walnuts, and pecans add variety, fiber, flavor, and healthy fats to the Mediterranean diet. Fresh oranges, figs, peaches, pears, and grapes provide a healthy alternative to sugary desserts plus antioxidants, vitamins, and fiber. Exercise also increases life expectancy.

Exercise and Aging. Exercise helps maintain strength, cardiovascular fitness, and mobility. The keys to maintaining fitness are consistency and alternating weight training with walking, jogging, cycling, or swimming to maintain strength, cardiovascular fitness, balance, and mobility. No one exercise will maintain strength and cardiovascular fitness; a variety of training methods is required. Avoid doing exercises that cause pain and perform training routines correctly to avoid injury. Alternating weightlifting with cardiovascular exercise is most effective because it allows the body to recover from different types of activities. Walking, jogging, swimming, or cycling three or four days a week for about forty-five minutes will improve heart health, promote elastic blood vessels, and regulate blood pressure. Another factor that increases life expectancy is social relationships.

Social Connections and Longevity. Humans are social animals, and having a network of family and friends helps people live longer. Studies show that maintaining social relationships significantly decreases the risk of suffering a heart attack, developing Type 2 diabetes, becoming depressed, or developing Alzheimer's disease. Living a long, healthy life requires developing and maintaining connections with friends and family, being embedded in a community, and feeling loved. Without social connections, people can become depressed, gain weight, develop Type 2 diabetes, suffer mental decline, and die at a young age. Unfortunately, opportunities for developing social connections have declined in recent years, so today people spend time alone, and report having fewer friends than earlier generations. Lacking connections to friends and family increases the risk of having a stroke by over 30 percent, raises the likelihood of developing dementia by 50 percent, and elevates the chance of dying by 20 percent. Social connections also foster productivity at work and lower turnover. The ability to develop and maintain social connections should be learned during childhood, but can be acquired at any age. Another factor that increases life expectancy is working longer before retiring.

Work and Longevity. Surveys suggest that nearly one-quarter of Americans aged 65 or older are still working, a significant increase from earlier generations. However, some employers view older workers as outdated, expensive, and set in their ways, rather than experienced, reliable and well-trained employees. Older workers can be valuable to a company because they have accumulated memories that will be lost if they are forced to retire at sixty-five. However, older workers must maintain their skills and technical knowledge if they want to remain employable in an evolving job market. Today, older workers are leaving company employment, establishing their own consulting businesses, and contacting with corporations to perform tasks as needed. If current trends continue, in another generation, freelance workers may outnumber corporate employees because they offer flexibility and lower costs to corporations. One concern among workers is that independent contracting is less secure than regular employment by a corporation, so individuals who choose to freelance need to have extra savings to tide them over slow periods of business. Another factor that increases longevity is being wealthy.

Money and Aging. Rich people live longer than the poor because they have access to better health care, eat a healthy diet, and live in more desirable areas. However, the relationship between money and longevity is complex. Being rich gives individuals access to better health care, advice on preventive health practices, and advanced medical technologies than poor people do. Wealthy people have a healthy diet, which increases their chance of living longer. Moreover, rich people can afford to live in safer communities, breathe cleaner air, drink clean water, and enjoy green spaces, which contribute to a longer life. Having a high income or inherited wealth also reduces financial stress, leading to longer, healthier lives. Also, wealthy individuals have access to more education which promotes healthy habits and better lifestyle choices. The gap in life expectancy between rich and poor has been growing in recent decades, so today wealthier individuals live even longer than the poor. There is no clear explanation for why low-income individuals who live in high income areas live longer than low-income families in poor areas. Perhaps they are influenced by the behavior of those around them or are forced to smoke less by local laws. Having money contributes to living longer, but it's not the only factor associated with longevity. Good genes and a healthy lifestyle also contribute to living a long and healthy life. If you want to live longer, choose your parents carefully, make healthy lifestyle choices, and visit your physician regularly.

Personal Experience. I changed my lifestyle after my father died at age sixty-two because I wanted to live a longer life. I was teaching psychology at the University of Illinois Urbana-Champaign, and began researching what was known about living a long, healthy life. I found Lelord Kordel's book, *Eat Right and Live Longer Look Younger Be More*

Vital, read it, and began a regimen of daily exercise, eating a healthy diet, saving and investing money, seeing a primary care physician annually for a physical exam, and spending more time with friends and family. I also discovered that eating a restricted diet, developing social connections, and having financial security help people live longer. My father had smoked from the age of sixteen and was overweight, while I never smoked and avoided gaining weight. To improve my lifestyle, I changed my diet, learned to relax, and began a health-oriented regimen I have followed for seventy years. It worked because I am ninety years old, financially secure, own a home, have a significant other who is supportive, and I survived prostate and colon cancer because they were detected early and treated effectively. I eat a Mediterranean diet, exercise daily, and hike four times a week with my daughter and grandchildren. I have no current health issues, weigh the same as when I was twenty-seven, have plenty of energy, my cognitive abilities and memory are intact, and I enjoy living. I recommend you take control of your life and follow a similar routine if you want to live a long healthy life.

ABOUT THE AUTHOR

HARRY MUNSINGER earned a BA from the University of California Berkeley, a PhD from the University of Oregon Eugene, was a post-doctoral fellow at Yale University, and earned a J.D. from Duke University School of Law. He was a college professor, clinical psychologist, practicing attorney, and expert witness before becoming a full-time author. Harry taught developmental and abnormal psychology at the University of Illinois Urbana-Champaign and the University of California San Diego. He has authored four college textbooks and published numerous psychology and law articles. Harry wrote nearly fifty articles for the *San Antonio Lawyer* and has published *Texas Divorce Guide, The History of Marriage and Divorce, History of Inheritance Law, and the History of Medical Miracles.* He has posted blogs that attracted national attention, Collaborative Divorce Texas established the Harry L. Munsinger Blog of the Year Award for the blog that attracted the most annual views, and Harry won that award the first year.

www.ingramcontent.com/pod-product-compliance
Lightning Source LLC
LaVergne TN
LVHW051006080826
845145LV00009B/2486

* 9 7 8 1 9 6 8 9 1 9 5 2 8 *